The Bee Cottage Story

How I Made a Muddle of Things and Decorated My Way Back to Happiness

Frances Schultz

principal photography by Trevor Tondro

foreword by Newell Turner

Skyhorse Publishing

Skyhorse Publishing books may be purchased in bulk at special discounts for sales promotion, corporate gifts, fund-raising, or educational purposes. Special editions can also be created to specifications. For details, contact the Special Sales Department, Skyhorse Publishing, 307 West 36th Street, 11th Floor, New York, NY 10018 or info@skyhorsepublishing.com.

Skyhorse® and Skyhorse Publishing® are registered trademarks of Skyhorse Publishing, Inc.®, a Delaware corporation.

Visit our website at www.skyhorsepublishing.com.

DESIGN
Janice Shay/Pinafore Press

Photographs by:
Trevor Tondro 2, 6, 9, 29, 64, 76, 77 (plates), 78, 80 ("after"), 82 (right, bench), 83, 86, 87, 94, 96-97, 98, 103, 104, 105, 129, 130 ("after"), 133, 134, 137 (left), 138, 145, 148, 149 (top right and bottom left), 150 (top), 155

Tria Giovan 81, 82 (left, fireplace), 84, 88-89, 99 (top),
142, 149 (top left)

James W. Reid 16 (wedding photo)

Courtesy Eleanor Larsen and John Jenkins 32 (Clark Family Photo)

Gina Stollerman 59

Missy Frey 146 (top)

Aaron Delesie 156

Anne Mayo Evans 158

Remaining photos were taken or provided by the author.

10 9 8

Library of Congress Cataloging-in-Publication Data is available on file.

Cover design by Anna Christian
Cover watercolor by Frances Schultz

ISBN: 978-1-63220-495-0
Ebook ISBN 978-1-63220-864-4

Printed in China

To Duvall, who knows the Bee Cottage story and all my other stories, too.
Thank you for listening, my darlin' sister,
I love you to the moon.

And to my husband Tom, our story is just begun.

Contents

He who loves an old house
   Never loves in vain
How can an old house
   Used to sun and rain,
To lilac and to larkspur
   And an elm above,
Ever fail to answer
   The heart that gives it love?

—*Isabel Fiske Conant*

Foreword

The editors of *House Beautiful* magazine have always believed in the power of home—not simply the value of owning a house but the satisfaction that comes from decorating and living in a beautiful, personal place.

When contributing editor Frances Schultz asked if we would be interested in doing a decorating story on a little house she had recently purchased, I immediately said yes. But at the time, Frances was only what I would describe as "occupying" the house. She hadn't really made it her own. Her visions for the rooms were just starting to take shape, and the spectacular outdoor living room was still on the drawing board.

We love a great story as much as we love a beautiful room. So, instead of waiting for a typical full-on, final ta-da feature, I asked Frances if she would share the renovation and decorating process through a yearlong column. Our readers loved it. Frances has a passion for decorating with the eye of an artist. She packed Bee Cottage, as well as the column, with so many great decorating tips and ideas. Honestly, her column became such a special part of the magazine that it left a gaping hole when it ended.

Little did I know, though, that Frances had much more to tell. And the full story is here. Like other great memoirists— M.F.K. Fisher, Frances Mayes, Elizabeth Gilbert, and Karen Blixen come to mind—Frances has written a book that is more than just another memoir. She tells a very personal story filled with experiences that are, for better or worse, universal and familiar to many. Most people would never expect that decorating a room and making a home could be therapeutic, even healing. But the renovation and decoration of Bee Cottage is a story about the pursuit of happiness through the art of decorating rooms and the power of making life pretty.

Newell Turner,
Editor in Chief,
House Beautiful

Bee Cottage before it became Bee Cottage. A bit run-down,
it had curb appeal but not much love. I felt a bit that way myself.

Chapter 1

A House, A Heartbreak, and How Did I Get Here?

Owning our story can be hard but not nearly as difficult as spending our lives running from it. —Brené Brown

I'd planned to make Bee Cottage the perfect place to begin my second marriage. I'd bought it with my fiancé's blessing. It was great for us and for his two sons. Though the house was old and needed work, I relished the prospect. If only I'd been as optimistic about the marriage, but the story of Bee Cottage begins, I'm sorry to say, with heartbreak.

After the wedding invitations were sent, after gifts received, after the ridiculously expensive dress made, after deposits paid, after a house bought . . . I called it off. I wish I could say he was a jerk and a cad, but he wasn't. He was and is a great guy. For purposes of our story I will call him G. The relationship failed because we just were not a fit.

And there I was with a house and the dawning that everything I had dreamed it would be would now be something else entirely. I cried, I hid, I hated myself. I stared at the walls, gazed forlornly at the non-existent garden, moped at the fifty-year-old refrigerator, sighed at the stove that didn't work, and fretted over the roof that needed replacing . . .

Looking back, I reckon many of us get to a place like this at some time or other, a spot that illuminates the space between where we are and where we thought we'd be. Sometimes an illness or loss jabs us into awareness of what we haven't done, where we haven't been, who we haven't become. But for many of us it isn't as clear as a single momentous event. It is more a culmination of experiences that turn out differently from how we expected— in a sort of climax of existential mission-creep.

In my Great Muddle of 2008, I had more questions than answers. One answer I did have, though, was that I loved this rundown little house with the blue shutters and the quirky rooms. I loved what it could be. I knew (more or less) what to do with it—more than I could claim in other areas of my life. I wondered if I could pull the house—and my life—back together at the same time. I would find love again, I told myself, and when I did I would give it a good home.

In my sea of fear, self-loathing, and self-doubt, amid heaps of mistakes and missteps, the belief that I could make the house lovely and welcoming, that this was something I might get right, gave me a glimmer of confidence and a glimpse of joy. My desire to create a beautiful, harmonious environment was a place of clarity for me in an emotional morass. Embracing that desire began to bring me around to who I was and what I could be. It was a point of light in a big dark room, but it was something.

Left: A grapevine-covered pergola off the dining room may have been original to the house, judging from the size of the vine's trunk. Right: The original kitchen door.

In many ways mine is the story of any decorating project, fraught with ups and downs and fits and starts. What surprised me was how the decorating process became both metaphor and means for personal discovery, and ultimately, for healing. I came to see how inherent in my love for decorating were the very insights and analogies that loosened the knots in my spirit. I think this holds true for everyone, be their passion for sport, art, literature, science, cooking, or teaching—whatever the calling, career, or hobby. All are rife with metaphors that point to our particular truths and what is authentic for us as individuals.

Like the Chinese saying about the longest journey beginning with one small step, so it was with Bee Cottage in beginning to hear my heart's song. This is the story of that process, soul-searching illustrated. I hope you'll find useful information here based on my years of experience with, and writing about, design for magazines, books, and my own blog, *FrancesSchultz.com*. I'm merely sharing my story and hoping something resonates with you if you find yourself in a similar place. Which I hope you don't. But if you do, whether it's a new house or a new chapter in your life (they often go together), my advice is to start from where you are, and begin with what you know. Because at the end of the day, that is all any of us have. And guess what? It's enough.

Left: There was a small brick terrace at the back. Right: Trees and hedges were overgrown and out of control.

Chapter 2

Childhood to Child Bride

I was born into a big extended family in a small Southern town. Our family was, and is, involved in farming, business, and some politics, and was prominent by our Tarboro, North Carolina, standards. My mother was a debutante and my father a dashing Army pilot. She had a thing for pilots. He had a thing for girls. It lasted long enough to have my sister and me. He had left the Army to return to Tarboro with my mother, but after they separated, he went back into the Army and pretty much out of our lives. This, I think, was my mother's preference, and suffice to say she had her reasons.

Mama remarried in 1969, again to a pilot, this time a Marine. We moved around a lot as military families do, returning to Tarboro during his 13-month tour in Vietnam,

Above: Age 2 and topless, Atlantic Beach, North Carolina, where we spent every summer growing up. Left: A handsome groom and his beaming bride, Trigg Brown and I just married and exiting the beautiful old Calvary Episcopal Church in Tarboro.

The reception was in the garden at home, with the cake in my mother's beautiful dining room, with silver foil-backed grass cloth on the walls and that wonderful Clarence House chintz. The chandelier was made by the erstwhile Edward F. Caldwell Co. in New York and is similar to those he made for the Rainbow Room in Rockefeller Center. My sister has it in her dining room today.

and returning again for good when he retired around 1978. By then I was away at school, the fifth generation of my family to attend St. Mary's School in Raleigh, North Carolina, and the first to go to the University of Virginia. (Everybody else had gone to UNC except Mama, who was reportedly given the choice between Duke and Vassar because Carolina was "too wild." She chose Duke undoubtedly to be nearer the wild.) When I was in my third year at UVa I met a tall, handsome boy, an alum and a few years older than I. I was mad for him. That he reminded me so much of my mother's brother, my Uncle "Dubba," was not lost on me either.

I was crazy about Dubba—everybody was. The quintessential Southern gentleman but with a twinkle in his eye that belied a glint of mischief, he was elegant but unaffected, part good ol' boy and part Cary Grant. As both my father and stepfather were absent most of my life, Dubba was my by-default paternal figure, and much beloved. I didn't consciously see my Virginia beau as a father figure, but Sigmund Freud would have. Anyway, we married the fall after I graduated and made our home in Richmond, Virginia.

Above: Age 3, I'm the little chub-by-legged one in the middle, as flower girl in my cousin and godmother Caroline Clark Trask's wedding.

One thing I never had to worry about was becoming a Rockette. I peaked at age 7 in Miss Bobbie's dance school in Tarboro, ca. 1964. I am the snaggle-toothed one second from left.

The year was 1980. I was twenty-two and saw myself as a career girl. Marriage wasn't on my agenda then, but he was ready, and he proposed. He also made it clear in the nicest way that if I said no, he would move on, and I didn't want to let him go. After six years we grew apart, and we did let go, in 1986. I adore him to this day. We rarely see each other, but we talk. He's been my stockbroker for thiry-five years. Twenty-five years after we divorced, he came to my mother's funeral. God bless him.

On a Grand Tour of Europe with my bestie Anne Louise Mayo Evans. No backpacks for us. Even as teenagers, we knew packing light was overrated.

From top to bottom: Sketching from a mokoro, in Botswana's Okavango Delta / Out for a ride on my sister and brother-in-law's farm in Newnan, Georgia./ Trekking in Nepal.

Chapter 3

The Single Years

After the divorce I wanted to spread my wings, travel, and be independent. For the next two years I did just that, making my way through Africa, Europe, Asia, and South America. It was wonderful, and I managed to eke out the odd freelance writing assignment now and again, while keeping journals and sketchbooks along the way. In 1989 I moved to Atlanta, and I lived there longer than I've lived anywhere until I moved to New York. Atlanta still feels like home when I visit, but I'd always wanted to live in New York. By then I was writing for *Veranda* magazine and they assigned me the title of "New York Editor," which I thought was pretty swell. So I went in 2000 and watched the Twin Towers burn a year later almost to the day. Something about that horrible day cemented me as a New Yorker and, I believe, brought all New Yorkers together in a way I haven't experienced before or since. Being there, living through that, was a defining moment for all of us.

Soon after I moved to New York, Turner South asked me to host their weekly TV show, *Southern Living Presents*, based on the popular magazine of the same name. Doing television was fun for me and came naturally, because I am a ham at heart. I loved it. The funny thing is I also kept writing for *Veranda*. It seems that every time I try to get away from writing, something happens to bring me right back to it.

On the romantic front, there were twenty-plus years of mostly serial monogamy spiced with the occasional madcap affair. (I once flew into the African Bush to meet a man from Texas on a hunting safari—for our second date.) With a few exceptions, my boyfriends were really good people. (Okay the hunter dude in Africa was a little crazy, but he didn't count as a boyfriend.)

Some of them proposed. I wasn't consciously avoiding marriage, but obviously some part of me was. Was I just avoiding commitment? Yes. Was I always looking for something better? Probably. Or for something that didn't exist? Also probably. Would I have known the right man if I'd tripped over him? Definitely not. Besides, I was having such a good time. Or so I told myself. And yet . . .

With so much good-time-having and devil-may-caring and on-and-off-airplaning, it is a wonder I ever got any work done. What is not a wonder is that I didn't know myself very well.

While I was out all those years making such an effort to be who I thought I was supposed to be, I forgot to be who I was.

I was so caught up in living an image of myself as the fabulous, achieving, intrepid Independent Woman that I didn't know who she was when the bags were unpacked and there was—God forbid—downtime.

I know there are women who've poured their energy into raising families while building careers who also emerge in their mid-forties feeling adrift, or like pieces of their soul had been pinched in the striving, the surviving, the success-making. They have families and communities to show for it (which I note not without envy), but they too pay a price. I had a well-worn passport, treasured experiences, malaria, and herpes.

While I was out all those years making such an effort to be who I thought I was supposed to be, I forgot to be who I was. Once when I lived in Atlanta one of the attendants at the vet where I sometimes boarded my dogs left me a phone message. She apparently thought she had hung up when she carried on talking to her coworkers . . . about me. Words to the effect of "She doesn't know who she is or what she wants, blah blah blah." Perhaps there was some jealousy involved. After all, here I was flying off to Paris or somewhere with what (to her) might have been enviable frequency. But I was none of her damn business, and who was she to judge me? Still, it

Above right: A one-sheet from a television show idea called Let There Be Style. *It never got past the pilot, but it was great fun doing it. Below: Atlanta gave me great opportunities and good press, too.*

Top: Lifeboat drill! Melissa Biggs Bradley, founder and CEO of the travel website Indagare; journalist Stephen Drucker, moi, and Karon Cullen, former head of public relations for Ritz-Carlton. We met on this cruise press trip around 1996 and remain friends to this day. / Below: At a friend's party in Portugal.

was hurtful to think I was perceived in this way by someone who knew me so superficially. And deep down, I suppose, I feared she had a point. I didn't know who I was, and I didn't know what I wanted. I was in such a whirlwind I couldn't feel the breeze. I'd created so much noise I couldn't hear my own heart.

From top left: Partying at the oasis. From left, my brother-in-law Rex Fuqua, sister Duvall, me, and Geoff Conroy at the Garden of Eden Ball that Duvall and I co-chaired for the Atlanta Botanical Garden in 1998. / As an on-air host for Southern Living Presents, *I got to do some pretty interesting things, like report from the White House press room. / Having traveled with the Sir John Soane Museum Foundation, I was recruited by board member Chippy Irvine (wife of the late designer Keith Irvine) to be in an 18th-century style maquette for the foundation's benefit in 2006. Chippy made the costumes from bubble wrap, trash bags, duct tape, pet food lids, and the like. What a hoot! With me is designer Leamond Dean. / Christmas in Newnan, Georgia, with sister Duvall and family circa 1995. From left, niece Frances, nephew John Rex, and niece Ruth. / Niece Isabel and our leopard slippers came a few years later.*

The irony is that I am, by nature, an introspective person. I'd just insisted on making self-understanding harder than it was. Where there was clarity, I made a muddle. When the road was smooth, I made bumps. But I'm good at tying bows and make a hell of a lamb stew. I can arrange flowers and furniture in my sleep. I can tell jokes. I'm artistic, and I'm a decent athlete. Some days I can even write. All those things are hints, by the way, to Who I Am, but back in the day I sometimes ignored my instincts and natural inclinations. I ignored my own authenticity, which I see now as a kind of slight to God, or Spirit, or Source, or however you call it. And it leads to nowhere good.

One of my favorite things to do while traveling is to sketch and paint. From top, windmill and garden folly in the German countryside; downtown Havana; and a restaurant in Normandy.

Chapter 4

Nowhere Good

Something about being in New York and dating New York men seemed to lead me to expect more and accept less. Something about being in New York, where it's all about what you do and less about who you are, began to erode my self-respect and my self-esteem with it. Everywhere I looked there was someone younger, smarter, wealthier, thinner, funnier, and prettier. I started thinking I wasn't nearly as fabulous as everyone else around me—especially those strolling along Madison Avenue and swilling martinis at posh parties.

The ensuing break-up was more damaging than I gave it credit for, but what doesn't kill us makes us stronger. It also makes us mad as hell.

Staying in romantic relationships past their sell-by date was long a pattern of mine. It came with the aforementioned territory and continued in my early New York years. *This is a perfectly good and nice man*, I would say to myself. *If I am really a good person, I will wake up one day and be in love with him like I should be, and be happy. And gosh, there are so few good men!* Oh, perhaps. But the truth is that I wasn't honest enough with myself to admit something or someone wasn't right for me, let alone didn't rock my world. *What had I done to deserve to have my world rocked?* When I finally did end a relationship I felt horrible, debilitating guilt. I was nowhere good.

Eventually nowhere good led to someplace worse: a relationship in which I felt diminished and objectified. The ensuing break-up was more damaging than I gave it credit for, but what doesn't kill us makes us stronger. It also makes us mad as hell.

He was the most famous person I ever dated. A highly visible and prolific television producer, he was well known in name if not in person. We met at a Christmas party and talked a while—a lot about his children and the perils of growing up with money, about his pending divorce. He didn't ask for my number and I didn't offer it. It never crossed my mind to be interested in him. So I was surprised when he called, and flattered. It's always flattering when someone calls. I'll be nice and go out with him, I thought, how bad could it be? He was, after all, smart, interesting, and successful. We'd have a great conversation, at worst. It turned out we had more than that—we had chemistry. Over the months I grew attached to him, more than I wanted to admit.

We'd been seeing each other for nearly a year.
He left my bed one morning and my life the next.

Now I am an independent sort, and not the jealous type—just the opposite, in fact. We saw each other on and off. He had a lot going on and so did I. When he was doing something or going somewhere and not including me, I didn't ask. Nice little Southern girl, I assumed he was busy and keeping a low profile as he was not yet divorced. What I missed was that he had a girlfriend on the West Coast all along. I ignored the creeping sense that he just wasn't Doing Right. Note to self: Don't ignore those creeping senses. They are never wrong. That I could have been so naive unnerves me to this day. And it's nobody's fault but mine.

The break-up was over a small thing, a bit of rudeness in an email. In my email back, I called him on it and a few other things while I was at it . . . about how he had the world on a string, and wonderful me with it, and how he deserved to be happy, etc. etc. I am brilliant at these sorts of tirades. His answer was, via Blackberry, "I need to get to a keyboard." And that was it.

We'd been seeing each other for nearly a year. He left my bed one morning and my life the next. I meant nothing to him. Nothing. I'd been ditched before, but not like that.

It was Thanksgiving. I went to the Ronald McDonald House in my neighborhood to serve Thanksgiving lunch. Being around children with cancer has a way of adjusting your perspective. I flew to London to be with old friends. Everything seemed better. I was sure I'd hear from him, if only to say "Hey, I'm sorry it didn't work out." But I didn't. Ever. Hear from him again.

When I returned to New York I heard he'd been hit by a truck. And you know what I thought? He needed to get hit by a fucking truck is what I thought.

When I returned to New York I heard he'd been hit by a truck while jaywalking. Someone sent me the item from *The New York Post*. And you know what I thought? He needed to get hit by a fucking truck is what I thought. I wished him no harm (well, maybe a little), but he needed to wake the fuck up. Pardon my French.

He recovered, by the way. The girlfriend came to nurse him back to health.

Some months later one of the doormen in my building asked me if I ever saw him anymore. Nope, I said. "That guy was an asshole," he said. It was soooo inappropriate. I burst out laughing. By then, I had bigger things to worry about.

Who am I to say someone else needs to wake up? When something goes off the rails in your life, the first thing you need to do is wake up yourself and look in the mirror. I'm the one who needed to get hit by a truck.

And I did.

Moody afternoon light under the grape arbor at Bee Cottage.

Chapter 5

The Big C

WHAM.

Cancer. January, 2004.

A routine mammogram revealed a tumor. (Get your mammograms, ladies!) Caught early and small, thank God, the little bastard was removed in a lumpectomy and the lymph nodes were clear. I was lucky. But it was an aggressive cancer called HER2/neu that the good folks at Memorial Sloan Kettering believed in treating with big guns.

"Big guns" is the technical term for The Next Year of Your Life is Going to Be A Huge Pain in the Ass. Oh, and your hair is going to fall out. Oh, and you will slam into menopause. Oh, and between the chemo, radiation, and drugs you're going to be taking for years, your body is going to change in ways they don't tell you about ahead of time or you'd be even more pissed off than you already were. Oh, and you're never having children.

Oh, and you'd better not let word get out about this or you're dead in this town. Oh, and you're alone . . . Who wants to hire a freelance writer who is so frightfully preoccupied? Let alone who would want to date one? So I kept my condition as much to my inner circle as I could. I also didn't want cancer to be what my life was about. I continued hosting *Southern Living Presents* for the erstwhile Turner South cable network and writing for *Veranda*, and I co-authored two books: *Signature Weddings* with Michelle Rago, and *A House in the South*, with Savannah College of Art and Design founder Paula Wallace.

Perhaps ironically, in some ways during that time I've never felt less alone. Cancer is a great teacher and, if you allow it, a great foil for silver linings. My friends and family were incredibly supportive. They did not hover, but they were there. I am not the type around whom people hover, and I am comfortable with a certain amount of solitude. Somehow, between my friends and my faith, I knew I would be okay. Something will get me one of these days, but it ain't this cancer, and it ain't now. I believed it, and I think they did too.

From top left: Do I look sick to you? Sporting my wig with old beau and good friend Jonathan Mermagen from London. We met in Capri to celebrate the end of chemo treatments. I was still bald as an eagle, so I slept in a little white knit cap. Jonathan said it was like sleeping with the pope. / All dolled up for my friend Bill Smith's birthday, 2004, not quite a year from diagnosis. I'd switched to a shorter wig so the transition wouldn't seem so drastic when my hair finally started growing back. / It does grow back. Here with my "chemo curls" and friend Alex Hitz in Venice. I had that big silk flower made to cover part of my cleavage. Not because of the surgery but because I am not Jennifer Lopez. / On a painting trip to Provence. I looked like a poodle.

Four generations of Clarks, ca. 1940. My mother,
Ruth Duvall Clark, is sitting on the ground in the
middle. / My mother and father on their wedding
day, 1955. They were married at mother's home in
Tarboro because it was my father's second
marriage and a church wedding was considered
unfitting. Have times changed or what. / Mother
with her brother, my Uncle Bill ("Dubba") Clark,
at a Tarboro shindig, ca 1960-something.
Tarboro knows how to shindig.

Chapter 6

Mama

The hardest thing about that whole cancer episode was dealing with my mother. We spoke every day, like we always had, she in Tarboro and me wherever I was. She was my best friend. And now my amazing, movie-star-beautiful, steel magnolia of a mama was getting old, and it did not suit her one bit. Health issues cropped up, overlapped, receded, only for others to appear. Not that she would *evah tawlk* about it to my sister or me, heaven forbid. She was still impeccably turned out, played bridge like a demon, and did the crossword in ink. But we sensed her disengaging, becoming less herself.

*The friend who'd been with her told me
Mama put on her lipstick before the ambulance came,
and when they asked her age, she lied.*

She and my sister came to New York for my surgery, and I was in and out in a few hours. I got dressed that night and went with my arm in a sling to the Plaza Athenée to meet them for dinner because it seemed easier than coping with Mama going out. What the hell, I was on Percoset. Why lie around the apartment?

But when she offered to come back to New York to be with me during a treatment, I begged her not to come. "I can't take care of you," I said, and I hated myself for it. Apart from the day of the bad mammogram—I knew it was bad that day—it was the only other time I cried that year. Way more than cancer and all its effects, knowing I was losing my mama, my best friend, broke my heart.

My biggest fear in life was being alone when she died.

By early winter of '04 my hair was growing back, in short, dark "chemo curls," they call it. I looked like a poodle. I'd begun seeing someone, a fellow writer, who had invited me to accompany him to Sri Lanka in December, where he would be researching his next book. It was an interesting trip, and he was a gracious host.

I returned home in time to spend Christmas with my sister, her family, and Mama, in Atlanta. My gentleman friend left two days after me in time to save his life, flying from Colombo to New York on Christmas Day and missing the tsunami of the century by hours.

I didn't know I was about to get a tsunami of my own.

That Christmas Eve at home we had a big crowd, like we always do. Mama sparkled as brightly

After Mother's second wedding to yet another military pilot, 1969, a few months before he left for Vietnam. She was still a babe. / At my beautiful sister Duvall's wedding to Rex Fuqua in Tarboro. As you can tell by our dresses it is 1989. That ginormous (faux!) sapphire and diamond necklace my mother is wearing with her Scaasi gown was on loan from her then-hairstylist, who was a cross-dresser. Some of the fancy people there from Atlanta asked her if it was a family piece. She said, "Sort of."

as the tree. After dinner she told story after story, maybe even a few we hadn't heard before (was that possible?), and we roared with laughter. Someone else would tell a story, and that would remind her of another one, and we'd roar again. God it was fun.

It was her last, best gift to us. The day after Christmas she couldn't get out of bed. She managed the next day to fly back to North Carolina. On New Year's Eve she went to the hospital. On New Year's night, 2005, she died, two months before her 74th birthday. The friend who'd been with her and called the ambulance told me Mama put on her lipstick before the medics arrived. And when they asked her age, she lied. That was Mama.

It was five or six years before I stopped reaching for my phone to call her every time I get in the car from the airport.

She never got to see Bee Cottage. I hate that. My love of houses, flowers, and pretty things comes from her.

Duvall, right, Mama, and me at a birthday party in Atlanta, 1999.

Chapter 7

Daddy

Meanwhile, over in Alabama, near the Fort Rucker Army base where he had worked, Daddy had been diagnosed with lung cancer.

But for a few of the seven years he was married to my mother and living in Tarboro, he was a career Army helicopter pilot and then a civil servant. My mother met him in Fort Bragg, North Carolina, where she taught English between parties at the officers' club (the real reason she was there). He was in the legendary 82nd Airborne.

My father was handsome, dashing, decorated, and brave. He was also a lifelong smoker. His idea of quitting smoking was smoking a pipe.

The marriage did not last, and because my mother was of independent means, she was not reliant on my father for support. Plus she was mad at him, understandably. So we grew up pretty much without him, without a history together. We saw one another occasionally, but a real bond never developed. The fault was nobody's and everybody's; it just worked out that way.

My father was handsome, dashing, decorated, and brave, having served in Korea and twice in Vietnam. He was also a lifelong smoker. His idea of quitting smoking was smoking a pipe. That's like a dieter quitting French fries for potato chips. As he neared the end and I visited him at home, he was still smoking that damn pipe.

The ashtray sat on the coffee table next to the pills and liquid morphine. The room was thick with smoke and awful, but also perhaps a last wisp of pleasure. I sat and mostly listened. He told stories about his hardscrabble childhood in Tennessee, how his father, an engineer for the Tennessee Valley Authority, drank a fifth of whisky a day and sometimes went after my daddy with a chain, or worse. He talked about my family and his time in Tarboro. He was well-liked there. He just wasn't very well-behaved, which he did not talk about. And he talked about Korea and Vietnam, the two times he was shot down, and how he missed getting the Distinguished Flying Cross because of a bureaucratic snafu. He took the bitter with the sweet and had a grand sense of humor.

I taped our conversation, hoping to piece together the chronology of a life I had not known. It was the reporter in me covering for the daughter and the raw sadness of a relationship that never was. But he had deteriorated by then, his memory and senses dulled by the blessed, obliterating opiates that eased his suffering. When his bony frame would shift on the sofa, and he'd wince, I'd say "Daddy, why don't you go ahead and take some more of that stuff?" And he said, "Have to be careful, Shug, that stuff'll kill you."

Two months later, in February of '06, he was gone.

The following spring, I met G.

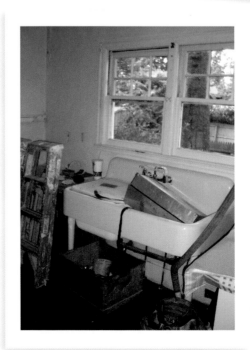

My first handyman special was nestled on a leafy lot in the village of East Hampton. I don't think a hammer or paint brush had been near it in quite some time, but I did love that old cast iron sink.

Chapter 8

Buying a House in the Hamptons

After years of being a houseguest in the Hamptons (thank you again, my dear hosts and friends), it was time to get my own place. An ad in a real estate magazine caught my eye: a small, shingled cottage on an acre-plus, right in the village of East Hampton. I bought it almost on a whim. I was in full-on cancer treatment at the time, so I blame it on the chemo.

Here, I thought, in the mess and fear of cancer, was something I could control, complete, and make pleasant—a little house. I've loved decorating since childhood, and though the process can be fraught, the prospects are a joy and the results a pleasure and comfort. Little did I know what the healing power of the process could be, both physically and emotionally. Surrounding myself with beauty, even in the simple forms of a well-ordered, aesthetically pleasing personal environment, is essential to my sense of well-being. Even when I was a little girl and we built forts in the woods behind our house, the rocks and sticks had to be lined up just so.

The house was a bit of a wreck. Believed to have been built from a Sears kit around the 1920s, the structure and interiors appeared to have progressed to about 1960 and slumped there. There was a black dial telephone in a niche on

Fresh paint and a few hydrangeas made a world of difference.

I used to worry about getting up at night and going down to the loo and falling . . . how the New York Post would write, " . . . days later she was discovered in a heap at the foot of the stairs . . . wishing she'd worn her good bathrobe . . ."

We planted lots of daffodils, which bloomed beautifully, and lots of tulips which did not. I was naïve then about the deer problem in East Hampton. Oy.

the stair landing and one of those huge cast iron sinks in the kitchen, which I actually loved. But the roof and exterior trim were in bad shape and the place suffered from sitting vacant for a year while the family I bought it from reportedly quarreled over estate issues. At the closing, nearly a year after I first signed the contract, several of the family members were in the room, glaring at one another. I kept waiting for somebody to reach across the table and grab somebody. Thankfully no one did (not then anyway), and finally it was mine.

The plan was to patch over the structural issues and decorate the house in "cheap and cheerful," while I designed my dream house to build elsewhere on the ample 1.3-acre lot. Paint and slipcovers carried the day, and the rooms were furnished with pieces I'd bought at my friend the designer Richard Keith Langham's tag sale and things I'd inherited from my mother. Atlanta designer and old friend John Oetgen, who'd guided

Below: How the large-scaled furniture I'd bought from designer and friend Richard Keith Langham's tag sale fit in this little cottage I do not know, but it did. I slipcovered most pieces in a Kravet cotton awning stripe. The botanicals I bought at the Paris flea market and the lamps from Target—but with custom shades. Right: I had curtains and a tablecloth made from burlap for the upstairs "study."

my Buckhead townhouse to an agreeable state of chic, helped me with fabrics and such.

The result was charming, albeit with drawbacks (there is only one bathroom, downstairs, while my bedroom is upstairs). I used to worry about getting up at night and going down to the loo and falling . . . how the *New York Post* would write, " . . . days later she was discovered in a heap at the foot of the stairs . . . wishing she'd

worn her good bathrobe . . ." But I knew the house was temporary, so it was okay.

We will not talk about the incident of the raccoons in the attic, but why no one has ever thought to send raccoons after terrorist groups is a mystery to me. They can destroy anything.

From top left: The kitchen sink got a striped skirt and matching awning above. Awnings are good solutions for dressing up windows with simple shades and nothing else. / A silly but economical shade for the kitchen light. / I painted the pantry and kitchen floor in a bright coral and white and trimmed the shelves in gingham.

A pretty slant of sun in the kitchen. I loved the coral and white painted floor.

Chapter 9

A New Beau,
an Old Pattern

I'd begun seeing G in the spring of '06. We were introduced by a mutual friend. He was attractive, smart, charming, funny, athletic, and beautifully mannered. He took me on a carriage ride through Central Park. If any girl tells you she doesn't fall for that kind of thing, she's fibbing.

My status as cancer vixen was intentionally not widely known and I always worried about telling people, because sometimes it can scare them. In a long, late-night talk when I was in Sweden on a Soane Museum trip and G was in New York, we crossed that threshold from superficial to serious, signaling our new relationship might become more than casual. I decided the risk of the cancer conversation was worth it. The next night I wrote him a long email, and held my breath.

Around lunchtime the next day, early morning in New York, he emailed back, simply, "I want to hear your voice." It was the sweetest, most loving answer I

The master bedroom. Left, half-canopy and coverlet in Michael Devine's Fretwork.
Carlton V pillows. Schumacher headboard and slipper chair.
Right, a ragtag collection of blue and white plates above a painted chest.

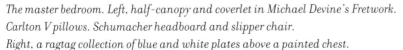

could have imagined. I nearly collapsed with relief right there in the middle of whatever Swedish castle I was visiting at the time, and I was endeared to G completely.

The two years or so I, and then we, spent in that first East Hampton cottage, I was pulling it together while at the same time working on new house

My mother's 18th century mahogany table got a coat of high-gloss white. Sacrilege, I know, but I didn't want a brown table. The two metal urn forms came from an antiques shop in town. I couldn't resist them. The beautiful shell photographs are by Nina Rumbough.

If my space is out of whack, then I'm out of whack. Admittedly I was not in the best of whacks to begin with.

Cheap and cheerful. Hardware store shelving with shells and starfish creates a focal point in the downstairs landing.

plans. Knowing it was temporary, I don't know why I couldn't be content more or less to camp out in the interim and not care how it looked, but I couldn't. If my space is out of whack, then I'm out of whack. Admittedly I was not in the best of whacks to begin with.

I ignored signs in my relationship that maybe it wasn't the best fit. Things I did and said in the course of just being Frances became points of contention. Innocent remarks became offenses. Those first few eggshells you walk on are sharp and crackly, but after that you get used to it. Your friends notice but don't tell you. What would they say? What could they say? G and I had become engaged.

There were of course ways in which we were well suited and comfortable together. I liked his friends, we loved playing tennis and golf together, and we both loved East Hampton. I used to tease G about proposing. He'd say, "Do you want to go get a hamburger?" And I'd say "Was that a proposal?" He'd say, "What movie do you want to see?" And I'd say, "Was that a proposal?" I thought it was hilarious, and he was a good sport about it, which I took as a sign he was open to the idea. Then one day on the tennis court, after we'd finished playing, he said "So you think we ought to get married?" I said, "That was definitely a proposal!"

I continued to work on designing the new house. I came to an impasse with one architect and began anew with another. By the time I started loving the design, we decided not to go through with it. It was going to be expensive (duh) and a touch grand for that particular block. Houses should belong to where they are.

We planned an April wedding. I told myself everything was okay, that the pit in my stomach was natural, nerves, stress, the strain of trying to get it all done.

The guest room was just big enough for a double bed. The pretty metal lit a la Polonaise was also from Keith Langham's tag sale. Bedding, Manuel Canovas.

Chapter 10

Another Loss

William Grimes Clark III, Bill, Uncle Dubba, in Nags Head, North Carolina, where various members of the Clark family have had houses since I don't know when. My 90-something cousin Teeny remembers having chickens and a cow right by the beach when she was a child.

March 30, 2008, was a Sunday, less than a month before the wedding. Planning had not gone all that smoothly and we were in Tarboro, where the wedding would take place, working through details. My cousins Rena and Louise were acting as wedding planners and floral designers, great at both.

Tarboro being Tarboro—population 10,000—ballrooms and banquet halls are scarce. We used to have a country club, but it burned down years ago and was never rebuilt. So we were standing in what used to be the corner gas station and auto supply store on Main Street discussing its merits as a rehearsal dinner venue. That a wedding six-plus months in the making for 250 people was a few weeks away and still not organized was not a good sign, and I had the knots in my stomach to prove it. The body does not lie.

I looked across the concrete-floored room to see Louise answer her cell phone. Her face contorted and her body slumped. "Dubba," she gasped. The sheer, heart-stopping incredulity of it froze any of us from reacting. My Uncle Dubba's dying was in the distant future, but not that day. With his wife Gray by his side as she always was, Dubba was at that moment in a fancy hospital suite at the Medical College of Virginia, watching ACC basketball and recovering from back surgery. Serious surgery indeed, but not something you die from. Unless a blood clot loosens itself from somewhere and goes to your heart and stops it.

Dubba was the last man standing who was close to us. He was handsome, funny, charismatic, and charming.

A diminutive of W for William, Dubba had been his nickname since college. My sister and I adored him. Safe to say our mother—his sister—adored him too, though not in a fawning way. With our father absent and former stepfather estranged, Dubba was the last man standing who was close to us. He was handsome, funny, charismatic, and charming. A consummate gentleman with not a pretentious bone in his body, he had no idea how many people considered him their best friend.

Not only were Dubba and Gray hosting our wedding reception at their home, but also Dubba was walking me down the aisle. I was even told part of the reason he had the damn back operation in the first place was because he wanted to feel good and to dance at my wedding.

There was a part of me that felt responsible for his death. That is absurd, I know, but I was about to make a pretty major mistake, which my mother would have seen coming a mile away . . . and I could hear her voice in my head saying, "Dubba, do something." *So maybe if I hadn't been such a clueless, stupid, bad person, I wouldn't have gotten in the situation in the first place, and maybe he wouldn't have died.* This is the worst kind of irrational fantasy, of course, but it left its tracks.

If there was a remotely conceivable silver lining, it was in postponing the wedding so G and I might sort out our relationship. We rescheduled the wedding for October, and we continued couples therapy. Note "continued."

Yes, we had been in therapy a while.

Above, Dubba and his wife, my beautiful Aunt Gray, on safari in Botswana, 1986. Trigg and I were lucky to go with them, my first of many trips there. Right, in 2006, celebrating Gray and Dubba's 50th wedding anniversary, our families went to Africa together, a magical trip.

Not to be rash, but if you're having issues that require therapy before you marry, maybe you ought to consider an alternative . . . like not marrying.

But I so much wanted to be a good girl, to do the right thing, to make it work, to fix myself so it would work. If I tried hard enough, I knew I could rearrange my thoughts and feelings to where I could make the relationship work. What was wrong with me?

Well, there was nothing "wrong" with me. I was just wrong for him. I see it now, but I didn't then.

What I saw was twenty years of being single, and that seemed like enough. I was tired of dating. Putting yourself out there to meet people and make plans is a hell of an effort at middle age. It's tedious going to a party or out on a blind date when you'd rather stay in watching *Downton Abbey*. Not that relationships don't take effort, but it's different. The last few years had wrung me out emotionally. My spirit was sagging. I wasn't just tired of dating, I was tired, period. In my Southern vernacular, I was wo' OUT.

Moreover, there was the stark fact of mortality. Having cancer and losing both parents and a precious uncle in one's forties does draw one's attention to the impermanence of life. I happened across this verse by Robert Frost:

Nature's first green is gold,
Her hardest hue to hold.
Her early leaf's a flower;
But only so an hour.
Then leaf subsides to leaf.
So Eden sank to grief,
So dawn goes down to day.
Nothing gold can stay.

So dawn goes down to day.

I looked at where in the day I was.

Why are we so often focused on what we don't have and what we haven't done? Why are we so stingy in giving credit to ourselves? I actually realized I'd achieved many of my career goals—writing for magazines, publishing several books, and hosting a television show, for example. But I'd missed some of the personal ones. Married and divorced in my twenties, I'd never had children. Being a mother was not a burning desire for me, but I took it for granted that I would be. Cancer treatment cancelled the possibility of motherhood, an ache I reckon will come and go all my life.

I was alone. I didn't want to be. I'd always been able to find a port in a storm. I had seen by this point, however, that life's storms could pick up my little boat and toss it on the rocks without warning. What I wanted now was safe harbor, and I'd chart a course from there.

The marriage was to be my harbor. So I hung in there with G.

Chapter 11

Finding the House, Losing the Marriage

The so-called "hanging in there" was rather a bleak combination of denial and obligation in which there is neither pride nor nobility. Nor common sense, for that matter. A bright spot, however, was the distraction of house-hunting. I love looking at houses.

When we pulled up to the stucco cottage on Fithian Lane, my pulse quickened a smidge. "I've had a thing for this house," I told G, excitedly. In fact I had seen the house a year earlier and was enchanted by its storybook charm and blue shutters. But prices in the Hamptons were at their most insane in 2007, and I wouldn't have dreamed of buying it then. However,

When a space is right for you, there is an instinctive response to it—an intuitive sense of how you would live there, where your things would go, what you would keep and what you would change. It's a project, but not a struggle.

2008 was a different story. The stock market had crashed and the financial world had collapsed. People selling houses in the Hamptons were a little bit gladder to see you.

The house was in an estate and had been vacant for more than a year, but the furnishings were largely still in place. An elderly man and his male companion had lived there previously. Before that the man had lived there with his wife, who had long ago retreated to upstate New

York. I learned later from a neighbor that the former wife was an English aristocrat—she was the countess or dowager countess of something—which perhaps partially explained the interiors. You could tell that those who lived there had style. The lines of the furniture, the cut of the curtains, the art—it all just felt right, dated and worn as it was. We could see ourselves there. "It has good joss," G said. We made the offer.

If it feels right, it probably is. If it doesn't, it isn't. Instincts are not wrong; ignoring them is. Worse is getting so off-track that you lose your instincts altogether.

When a space is right for you, there is an instinctive response to it—an intuitive sense of how you would live there, where your things would go, what you would keep and what you would change. It's a project, but not a struggle.

Why couldn't I see that in my personal life as well? An analogy both obvious and simple, how could it be so clear with a house and not with a man? In a way they both entail important, intimate relationships. If it feels right, it probably is. If it doesn't, it isn't. Instincts are not wrong; ignoring them is. Worse is getting so off-track that you lose your instincts altogether.

My heart had so many ifs, buts, and shoulds wrapped around it that I barely recognized it. The relationship with G did not feel right and had not for a while.

The one thing that did feel right was this house, and I took comfort there. That search was over.

Elsewhere in my life, another search continued.

Celebrating the closing with then-real-estate agent and still-friend, Frank Newbold.

Bee Cottage as I found her in 2008, with a somewhat overgrown yew hedge and ivy growing up the walls.
As we found it, the house had been lived in until recently by an elderly couple with quiet good taste.

Chapter 12

Seeking a New Path

The week I received the cancer diagnosis, a seemingly random encounter would become one of the most important of my life. I was with friends in a restaurant, and as the evening wore on we lingered at the bar. I found myself in conversation with a stranger, and no, he wasn't hitting on me. But you know how you'll tell a stranger something you wouldn't tell a friend? I told him about my diagnosis. He told me his mother was a healer. It was like an angel landed on my shoulder. I called her the next day.

We met in her office, and she asked me if the tumor was in the upper left quadrant of my left breast. I had not told her, and she had not seen test results. "Yes!" I said, "and you should be on TV!" A practitioner of the Barbara Brennan School of Healing, Anna Schalk and I worked together for three years. I am certain she is one of the reasons I did so well during those cancer treatments and later was able to navigate the numbing grief of my mother's death.

As our energy work progressed it became less about the body and more about the spirit. I was honored when Anna referred me to her teacher, who had progressed from medical nurse, to energy healer, to spiritual teacher. She had developed a three-year course called "Awakening Into Presence" based (mostly) in Tibetan Buddhism. Entailed were four weekend workshops per year, as well as weekly telephone sessions, and twice-daily meditation practices. It was a serious commitment. I had meditated off and on since college, but the practice I began then I continue to this day. If you can be an Episcopalian Buddhist, I suppose that is what I am.

At one of the workshops, a fellow student and wonderful soul named Cheryl recommended to me a book called *Sacred Choices*, by Christel Nani. A former emergency room nurse and a medical intuitive, Christel can clairvoyantly "see" physical illness or injury in the body. An-

The labyrinth at Canyon Ranch, Tuscon, Arizona

other of Christel's books, *Diary of a Medical Intuitive*, chronicles these experiences and how she eventually, if reluctantly, left the ER to be an energy healer and teacher.

I didn't so much read *Sacred Choices* as inhale it. It affected me so that I could literally feel its energy running through me. That sounds so weird, I know. It *was* weird, to be honest. In addition to her own story, Christel recounted those of her clients, all in situations not right for them but in which they stayed in loyalty to a "tribal belief." This is a belief that may once have served to preserve the "tribe," but that had ceased to serve the individual. A woman holding the tribal belief that "marriage is forever no matter what" might stay in an abusive relationship despite the damage to herself and her children. Not good. Another example: "All the Jones men are engineers," is a fine tradition and had served the family well. But what of the

It was clear and simple. Take responsibility for your circumstances. Own your talents and God-given gifts. Speak your truth.

son who really wants to be a teacher? Instead, Son follows the tribe, and twenty years later he's in a slump and doesn't know why. Christel might say it's because his energy wasn't behind his work, because he was not living his "energetic blueprint." He's not being who he was born to be, and that is not good for anyone. The same principle applies to relationships.

Of course I am super-simplifying something that occupies an entire book, but this is the gist: It is possible for disease in the body to begin energetically, in the chakras. Chakras are the body's energy points representing aspects of our being, from personal safety to self-esteem. Weakening the energy, can weaken the spirit, can weaken the body. The idea that strong self-esteem is good for you is not new news, but Christel's advice about energetic wellness was not touchy-feely; it was clear and simple. Take responsibility for your circumstances. Own your talents and God-given gifts. Do what you love. Speak your truth.

Talismans and reminders: The word "authenticity" is taped to my computer, and the laughing Buddha was a gift from a beloved teacher.

My takeaway was profound excitement that we have energetic blueprints, and that we could live by them, even though it might mean going against the tribe. I had a nagging feeling I wasn't living my blueprint, and I wanted to do something about it, whatever that meant.

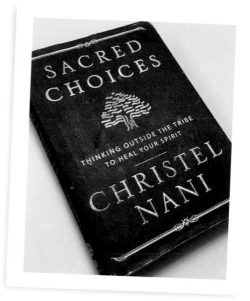

Meanwhile the situation with G deteriorated. It's like I was living two lives. There was my spiritual life wherein I felt clear, at peace, and optimistic in my meditation and studies, and my life with G, where I felt confused, inadequate, and at fault for whatever wasn't going right. But I couldn't admit that, or the whole thing would fall apart. Which of course it did.

After an initial burst of hopefulness with our counseling, things went sideways and then down.

Christel Nani was conducting a weekend workshop in Albany, and I went. Certainly a part of me was hoping for reassurance that no relationship was perfect and that mine

Subtitled "Thinking outside the tribe to heal your spirit," Sacred Choices by Christel Nani changed my life.

was as okay as any. I was hoping I had not made a shambles of my life, even though it sure felt like one. And if it wasn't a shambles, well, that wasn't too good either. How screwed up is that?

I was impressed with Christel. She was a no-nonsense New Yorker with a credentialed medical background, a sense of humor, and compassion without the kumbayah, to my relief. Near the end of the first day she asked for volunteers to tell her one thing they really loved doing or wanted to do, have, achieve, or change. It had to be something our energy was behind 100 percent. It had to register all the way down to our toes and come all the way back up again, to sail effortlessly through every chakra. It didn't have to be anything profound. It could be "I really like chocolate." Sounds easy, right? I was shocked by how many people couldn't do it.

I raised my hand. I got this, I thought. I'd just bought Bee Cottage. It was the one thing in my life I felt I knew my way around. So I said, "I want to create a warm, wonderful home and garden where my friends and family can gather."

"No . . . " Christel said. Wait, wha . . . ? My quizzical, embarrassed look said it for me. She continued, "Do you want to write a book about . . . ?" And I interrupted her, if you can believe. She's about to reveal something really important—the reason I came here—hello?—and I interrupted her. Typical.

"Well that's what I do," I said.

"Do what?" she asked.

"I write books and articles and things"

"Oh," she said. And that's all I remember. It sort of ended there. I was completely flustered and felt like a jerk. I don't know if she was going to say anything about my relationship, but it's all connected. If you limp around on a sore ankle, eventually your hip starts to hurt, then your back, and so on. Our spiritual health is the same.

I just didn't know what to fix. Everything felt broken and I didn't know where to start.

Christel's whole thing is about how tribal beliefs hold us back: *Relationships are hard work. Blood is thicker than water. You must earn everything you get.* Etc., etc . . . I'm not saying there isn't validity in all of them, but they are beliefs, not facts, and there's a difference. I wasn't in an abusive relationship or a miserable life. I was with a good guy and in a nice life. So what right did I have to complain? *Get a grip*, I told myself. *You've got it all. What's wrong with you?*

Whoever we are, if we are in a situation that is demoralizing, it is ultimately going to be unhealthy as well. Feeling guilty or getting sick isn't going to make anybody else better, richer, or happier, so what is the point? Serving a tribal belief to our individual detriment is to sacrifice our self-respect.

The walking on egg shells in my relationship had to end. My fear of anger and disapproval served no one. Staring into space at four in the morning with knots in my stomach was neither healthy nor character-building. And yet I was so paralyzed by the implications of my doubts that I could not acknowledge them.

I never got the big "aha" I was hoping for at the workshop, but I did see a new possibility. I made a plan: The next angry impasse G and I came to, I would simply remove myself. Gently but firmly, I would say something like, "We seem to be at tough spot, and we are both upset. I need to be alone now to calm down and collect my thoughts. Afterwards I will be better able to discuss this with you."

My chance to try it out came soon enough, and the end came soon after.

There is never a good time to break up. There is always an element of the surreal about it, and a part of you that can't believe it is happening. The other part of you puts one foot in front of the other and carries on, while your head and your heart flounder for closure that never truly comes. Lives once shared have a common history that cannot un-happen.

Several months later on a Sunday in October, I was supposed to have dinner with someone a friend wanted me to meet, which I wanted to do about as much as I wanted to go to the dentist. Oy, but you have to start somewhere.

Six years later I am still having dinner with the handsome guy waiting for me that night at the corner table in La Goulue, but I'll get to that in a little bit.

*Exploring the energy vortexes in Sedona, Arizona.
Above, on a hike to the ancient Wind Caves. Below,
Watercolor by moi, somewhere in Arizona*

Chapter 13

Detour

As if I hadn't taken enough wrong turns already, I may as well tell you that while I was at it, I also committed to a job I wasn't right for. I know. It's almost funny at this point.

After twenty years of happily writing about design and entertaining for *House Beautiful*, *Veranda*, and others; composing several books; doing on-air hosting of *Southern Living Presents*, and appearing at speaking gigs far and wide, I fizzled. My writing lost its sparkle, and so

I am fifty, honey. You'd think I'd have gotten by now the part about following your heart and being true to yourself, but no.

did I. In thinking I needed a change, I accepted an attractive offer in the fashion business. In the precarious economic environment of 2008, a regular paycheck and benefits—two things I hadn't had in years—were a compelling attraction, I confess. Besides, I've always loved clothes, so why not?

Well, I love fires too, but that doesn't mean I should be a fireman.

Now remember I'm not twenty-five at this point, or even thirty-five. I am fifty, honey. You'd think I'd have gotten by now the part about following your heart and about being true to yourself, but no. My truth was a blur. You might not have known it to look at me—hell, I didn't know it myself—but I was a mess. I'd gone flat, and it seemed my life had gone flat, too.

I'm not ashamed of that. We all have bad days, bad years, even. What I'm ashamed of is believing I deserved it. I believed I had deserved it for leaving a good guy, for being dissatisfied with a good job, for stealing a pack of Lifesavers from the Piggly Wiggly when I was seven. You name it. With so many transgressions, how did I possibly deserve happiness?

Well, where is it written that you must deserve happiness in order to have it? Or that you must earn every single blessing in your life? Precisely nowhere, that's where. These were my own twisted, albeit unconscious, interpretations of what Christel Nani would call typical tribal beliefs—something along the lines of *Success and happiness must be earned through hardship,* and *Some mistakes are unforgivable.*

I trusted my grief would ease and my body would mend; it was my spirit that needed healing. And meanwhile, in a village on Long Island, sat a house needing love. The truth is that we needed each other.

Bianca, my bicycle, parked at Bee Cottage.

Chapter 14

How Bee Came to Be

Away from the honking hustle of New York City, this house, like the one before it, would be a place where I could recover, be creative, be outdoors, be cocooned, be social, be alone, and best of all, be me, just . . . be. And that's how it got the name Bee Cottage. I like the play on words, and I also like bees, which, after all, are creative, hard-working, focused, social, drawn to beauty in flowers and trees, and have a queen. I like all that. So, I told myself, you've survived the big C, the deaths of your closest loved ones, and a public humiliation. You've got on your conscience hurting someone you cared about deeply. Now what?

As children we'd dig holes on the beach, believing if we kept digging we'd get to China. And that's what I was thinking, I'm about to hit China. But I didn't. I stayed right where I was. Stop digging and be, honey. Just bee.

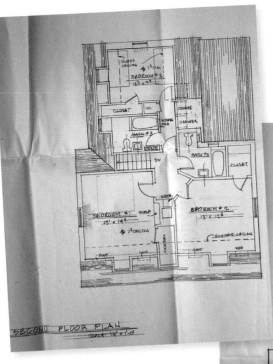

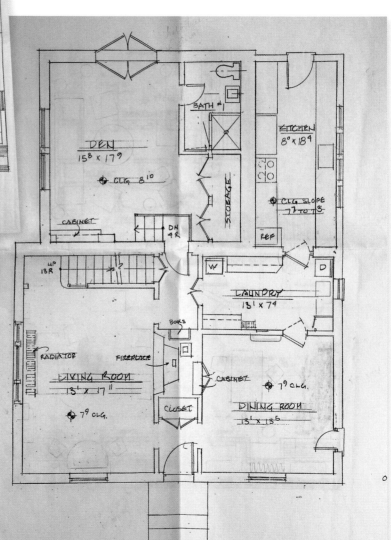

The floorplan as it was, and is.

Chapter 15

You Have to Start Somewhere

Whether you are beginning a new design project or a new life chapter—or both, ahem, as does happen—the hardest part can be taking the first step. You know you have to start somewhere, but where exactly? The short answer is right from where you are.

Remember when you were in school and took standardized tests? They always said if you came to a question you couldn't answer, skip it and move on to the next. Same with a puzzle, do the easy parts first. That makes the hard ones much easier to fill in later, and sometimes they fill in themselves. So it is with re-doing a house, and possibly with mending a heart. Start with what you know. I did know I loved this house, so I started with that.

As with any major undertaking, if you break it into parts, it is considerably more manageable. And in case you missed it the first twenty times I said it, if you begin with what you know, you'll have a starting point. So here's what I knew: The nice thing about small, asymmetrical rooms and ceilings you can touch without standing on tiptoe (I'm 5'10", but still) is that there are only so many ways to go. This house, as the real estate agent kept saying, "is what it is." That is, a little 1920s East Hampton stucco cottage that had suffered neglect, but not abuse. Previous owners were respectful of the cottage's modest charms and had done nothing to dampen its cheerful and cozy spirit. So I guess my first decision was to preserve that. No knocking out walls or ceilings or re-arranging the floor plan. We'll work with what's here and find a way for it to work with us. And with that, Bee and I were on our way.

Chapter 16

First Steps:
From the Outside In

Architectural historian Grant Hildebrand talks about buildings offering "prospect" and "refuge," concepts he says apply even to the humblest of dwellings. Like this one. It seems a vaunted theory for a simple old house, but to understand it is to know immediately why you feel comfortable in one house and uneasy in another. It has nothing to do with the size of the house, but we humans desire areas that offer possibility, views, and the "prospect" of discovery and expansion; while conversely we also need areas in which we feel protected and safe—"refuge." Lord knows I needed refuge, as do we all at one time or another. In their humble ways, the rooms of Bee Cottage embody these principles of prospect and refuge, hence the house's intuited good joss—and a way home for my heart.

The house's village location was ideal. It would be nice to feel surrounded by people and activity, and I would be less likely to brood. My brooding tendency was high at the time, to say the least, and loneliness was a big gray lump in the middle of every day.

My former fiancé and I had agreed that a wonderful garden was a priority, and landscape plans were underway almost as soon as the sale closed. I would also add an outdoor living and entertaining space—the better to enjoy the garden. He had not wanted a pool; I had. Calling the garden designer and asking her to put in a pool was a small act of post-breakup defiance that was ever-so-subtly empowering.

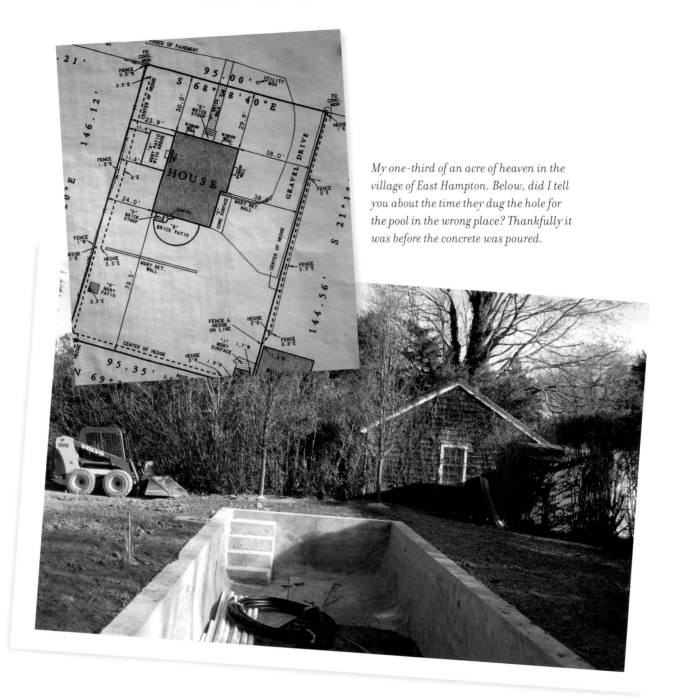

My one-third of an acre of heaven in the village of East Hampton. Below, did I tell you about the time they dug the hole for the pool in the wrong place? Thankfully it was before the concrete was poured.

How to Begin – Finding Your Vision

Before you do anything to a house, try to decide how you're going to live in it. Presumably you have a fairly good idea of your day-to-day habits. List them, if you find it helpful. From waking in the morning until going to bed at night, how do you move through the rooms of your house or apartment, and how do you and your family use them? It might be helpful to keep a log of these activities just to make you aware of them. So much of our behavior is habitual or unconscious that sometimes we find that the perception of it differs from the reality. For example we may think we entertain often, or would like to, but in truth it's more like twice a year. Plan to organize your space around what you really do, rather than what you think you should do.

Don't expect all your ideas to come at once, or all of them to remain in place. Give yourself flexibility, particularly in the planning stages when changes cost nothing.

Something about the dynamic of the relationship had kept me in don't-rock-the-boat mode, feeling slightly squelched. Those who know me might not think of me and "squelched" in the same sentence, by the way. So what if an un-squelched me had spoken up earlier in the relationship? What would have happened? Either the relationship would have developed on sounder, stronger footing with two people being true to who and what they were; or it would have ended sooner. Either of which would have been preferable, obviously, to speaking up as late as I did. Not being yourself does no one any favors, especially not you. But I was afraid that myself wasn't good enough, that my judgment was inferior.

By coming to an understanding of what was right for my house, I came to a better understanding of what was right for me, period. I believe this is universal, by the way, and the more

A metal chalkboard in the kitchen is used for menus, messages, and silliness.

conscious we are of how we shelter ourselves, both literally and figuratively, the more conscious we are of ourselves.

The house, just as it was, held lots of appeal. What I wanted was just to make it a better version of itself. In the state I found it, Bee's exterior stucco was weathered and ivy-strewn, with shutters that were the most wonderful shade of blue. Whoever picked that blue was a genius. What was not to love? Well, I'll tell you.

On closer inspection, landscaping in the front comprised all of a scraggly yew hedge, and at the side an overgrown arborvitae arching densely across the driveway, so when you passed through it you felt you might enter a magic forest. Or a money pit. The roof was asbestos and old. The front door was feeble, but its top two panels were the original bull's-eye glass—charming. The driveway was patchy and weedy.

Fortunately, estimable garden designer Jane Lappin had a keen sense of the appropriate, which is important in a historic town like East Hampton. Boxwood replaced the yew in an intentionally random-looking arrangement. A low boxwood hedge in front creates a formal frame. Boxwood and ilex hide the hideous gas and electric meters that had to be placed where they could be easily read. Some plans are dictated by aesthetics; others by necessity.

Because of the pool at the back, the area around it had to be entirely fenced in, which then needed screening, and front and back gates. Two of the three gates have bee cutouts, designed with the help of Jane's associate

Bee Cottage in its original state, with the shutters whose color I'd feared I couldn't replicate.

The garden gate bee design appears also as an appliqué on linens and as a design element on stationery and on FrancesSchultz.com

Adrienne Woodduck. That same bee design has since been used on linens, stationery, and on my website. When you find a good bee, buzz it, I say.

Window boxes and cottages just go together, and this is a window-box-y house if ever there was one. So, okay, up with the window boxes.

I hated the expense of replacing the roof, but it was necessary, and the new cedar shake shingles are a world of difference.

The arborvitae got a serious trim so the workmen could drive their serious trucks by it. The living room windows on that side now let in a lot more light. I had actually liked that overhanging arch, but there you go. The area adjacent is now planted with oakleaf hydrangeas, which are also good as cut flowers to use in the house.

There was no way around replacing the front door, although dang I hated losing that bull's-eye glass . . . So I didn't. One pane had been broken, but we were able to replace it through a source I found on the Internet. Soon the front door was restored to its good-new-old self, but better. We stained it a dark walnut and coated it with polyurethane to give it polish and gloss, like you see in English townhouses.

Oh, and the shutters? I get at least ten questions a year about the color. I was able to match it exactly, using Benjamin Moore's Mountain Laurel.

The interiors were to have been pretty much my domain from the beginning, so no big post-breakup adjustments there. The major projects were the kitchen and butler's pantry, which I was happy about because I cook and entertain a lot and so could design them to suit.

Left, before, the overgrown arborvitae formed an arch over the driveway: poetic but impractical. Right, from the opposite side, with the tree trimmed and old hedges removed, the space opens up dramatically.

As much as form follows function, I confess I did not have all the function figured out at first. When I moved in at summer's end of 2008, it was with boxes of uncertainty about the house, the future, and ever finding happiness. At least in the decorating I could start with a few decisions and work up to the rest. I told myself just to wait, to let design solutions come. Maybe other solutions would present themselves as well. The house was becoming a metaphor for my life. I kept seeing parallels between fixing up the house and facing my now-upended life, and I wondered if the house was a way toward healing.

It took a year to figure out how all the spaces should work. In the meantime I crept forward with filling in other answers I knew, like paint colors and arranging the living areas.

AC-20

mountain laurel

Above, the blue shutters today: Benjamin Moore's Mountain Laurel, on the nose. Right, the front door's bulls-eye glass is a subtle, old-fashioned detail worth preserving.

The color palette was determined by complex criteria: It had to go with the stuff I already had. And while the colors—sea-grassy greens; cool blues; a touch of gray; and a warm, luminous white—aren't exactly breaking news for a beach house, they all resonate with sea, sand, and sky, and are quiet and calming. That surely would be conducive to healing.

Another inspiration came from these wonderful plates I bought several years ago at a little shop in Sag Harbor. The pattern is blue and softly splattered like a robin's egg, with gray-ish, brownish feathers painted on. I was besotted with them and had always wanted to do a room around them.

So the living room fireplace niche, stairway, and one bedroom would get that particular egg-y blue. All doors and window mullions were painted a high-gloss gray, which was a unifying element throughout the house. Painting mullions a darker color seems to diminish the boundary between inside and out. A value similar to the scenery beyond makes the view more continuous, while a light color stops your eye and draws your focus to the window itself.

Notes on Curb Appeal

Boring but important: Roofs are to houses what shoes and bags are to dresses. Have the best you can afford, and the whole outfit looks better. Gutters are the earrings. Copper would have been swell, but it's become so expensive that vandals might steal it and sell it for scrap. What about just plain old zinc, suggested my designer friend Tom Samet, who was right as usual.

Have a great, solid front door. Bee's original was worn out, but I loved the two bull's-eye panes at the top. I had a new door made to accommodate the bull's-eye glass, then stained and polyurethaned the wood for permanent luster. It looks handsome and substantial.

If something is old and you think they don't make it anymore, ask anyway. An original pane of bull's-eye glass in the front door was accidentally broken. I wept as I Googled and lo! Resources galore.

Just because it's old doesn't mean it's good, but sometimes it is.

Sometimes new is better, though. Scraping and putting down new gravel on the driveway, for example, is like giving the house a new, well, driveway.

The reflective quality of the high gloss paint is just great, especially in a place where the light is beautiful, as it so famously is in East Hampton. I've always heard that high-gloss finishes should only be used on walls in perfectly pristine condition, and I've always ignored it.

Left, The grape arbor off the dining room would remain as it was. The light filtering through the vines is downright poetic. Above, re-doing a house is a list-maker's idea of heaven . . . or hell . . . I'm not sure which.

76

These paint-spattered, be-feathered Robin's egg blue plates were the touchstone of Bee's color scheme. Top right, clockwise from top, Mountain Laurel, Galapagos Turquoise, Tudor Brown, Wedgewood Gray, Kiwi, Davenport Tan, Palladian Blue, Shale, and Powder Sand, all Benjamin Moore. Below right, the kitchen scheme.

Chapter 17

The Living Room

The original living room had a fireplace and would lend itself to nesting and gathering on chilly winter nights. I've spent many nights there having dinner at the little table and then curling up with a stack of books and a glass of wine. And while this is one of my places to cocoon, it is also where I entertain in winter.

At 13 by 17 feet, the space isn't terribly large, and there are other features to contend with, namely a radiator, two windows, three doorways, and a fireplace. It seems small when empty, and yet it is surprisingly accommodating, comfortably seating seven or eight.

Removing the doors leading to front and back vestibules cut some of the visual clutter. A third passageway leads to the stairs, and we capitalized on the niche at the landing at the foot of the stairs by building shelves for some of my Staffordshire collection.

To anchor the room I placed an armless banquette I'd acquired at designer Richard Keith Langham's tag sale. It was perfect opposite the fireplace, even though it's against the radiator. The streamlined silhouettes of banquettes and slipper chairs are especially good for small spaces and always look chic. My slipper chairs were nothing special, but they were about the only things I could afford in the Sotheby's auction of Katharine Hepburn's estate. They were frayed and beat to hell when I got them, a state that I thought enhanced

View of the living room from the front door entrance. A pair of Swedish chairs from designer Tom Samet flanks an old family Victorian game table. Painted cabinet long in my collection holds porcelains I can't seem to part with. Vintage bee print and bee keep atop cabinet.

Top, the living room as it was before. Above, living room in the interim. The slipcovered Richard Keith Langham-designed banquette came from my previous house and remained "as is" for a while. The pair of club chairs I bought from the owner's estate and re-covered. Lamps are re-purposed antique Italian candlesticks.

Opposite: The Living Room today, with the banquette re-upholstered in a textural geometric woven that works well year-round. The pillows are always being moved around.

their WASPy, shabby glamour. Eventually I relented and re-upholstered the chairs and the banquette in a cozier, more wintry fabric, saving the striped cotton slipcovers for the warmer months. (The slipper chairs have since migrated to the garden room, replaced by re-furbished chairs of my mama's.)

It is such a lovely thing to change your rooms with the seasons, putting crisp cotton slipcovers on wintry upholstery. Admittedly somewhat of an extravagance, slip-covering does extend the life of upholstery by sparing it wear and tear.

For warmth and texture we glazed the walls a soft caramel and added a honey-colored sisal rug. Curtains, pillows, and cashmere throws are the final layer of "soft goods."

A painted cabinet stores china and decorative objects, which I rotate in and out. A mahogany Victorian table can be used for dining à deux or unfolded for cards and games. The two chairs flanking it can also be pulled up to the conversation group around the sofa when company comes. It's a surprisingly lot of stuff for a small room, but it functions well.

The enormous bronze dolphin chenets flanking the fireplace no doubt made sense in the Newport mansion they likely originally hailed from, and they were grand and beautiful in my mother's library in our big old family house in Tarboro. But in a stucco cottage across the street from a grocery store parking lot, they find themselves in rather reduced circumstances, I'm afraid. In the meantime they have been made into beautiful lamps, but they can easily reclaim their former glory should their fortunes change.

Inset above: The fireplace before . . .
. . . and now. The armchairs by the door have hence migrated here. Lamps are re-purposed bronze fireplace chenets that were my mother's.
At right, a narrow antique English church bench is a landing strip for magazines, pocketbooks, and what all. Photograph of the sea is by my dear friend Holger Eckstein.

The niche and stairway were painted in a pale robin's egg blue. The lampshades are trimmed in gross-grain ribbon and sea shells—an easy DIY. Shallow shelves hold a collection of Staffordshire and create a focal point.

Chapter 18

The Garden Room

What I call the garden room had once been the garage, and because it has the best light and views of any room in the house, this is where we would hang out—particularly in the mornings and in the warmer months.

So that's where I put the television and the Sofa That Ate Long Island. My friend, designer Richard Keith Langham, had a tag sale a few years ago and I scored this fabulous HUGE sofa. It is 10 feet long and 4 feet deep. I must have been thinking I would save it for when I moved into Windsor Castle. Anyway, there it was and it was fine. It's definitely comfy. You can hardly get out of the thing once you're in it. It worked well with other Keith cast-offs, over-scale arm chairs, and an over-size wing chair we call the Edith-Ann chair.

(For those old enough to remember the television show *Laugh-In*, comedienne Lily Tomlin's little-girl

Opposite: An old chaise is given new life in a Mauel Canovas linen print. Note: I firmly believe that every place to sit also needs a light and a place to put down a book or a drink. And P.S., you can hang pictures almost anywhere, even on the side of a banister.

Above: Previous owners had converted the garage into a living area with the advantage of the only "public" room besides the kitchen that opens onto the terrace and garden. Below: A small set of stairs leading into the room has the effect of adding another bit of wall space.

character Edith Ann would sit in this enormous chair with her legs sticking straight out and impart her wisdom, always ending with "And dat's de twoof," then sticking out her tongue and making a poot kind of noise, like a whoopee cushion. I still think it's funny.)

Compared to the rest of the house the garden room was practically a ballroom, with ceilings soaring up to 8 feet and a nice, almost square proportion. It seems counterintuitive to put a sofa and chairs so big in a room that size, but large-scale pieces can make small rooms seem bigger. I swear.

The wallpaper is graphic and bold, a departure from the more muted tones in the rest of the house. It gives the room a sense of destination, like a special but separate part of the house. Love a trellis, always have. So fresh and garden-y. It also worked with the old green striped slipcovers and is just as good with the later addition of a floral print. Geometrics have a way of accommodating both prints and solids and are always a great way to spiff up a room.

Sometimes you have to be willing to let a room surprise you, and also to let it change. Our rooms evolve as our lives

Above: Painting the backs of bookcases makes what's in them more interesting. On the top shelf are a collection of Italian terra cotta pots that are mementoes from New York Battery Conservancy benefit luncheons over the years. Miniature gilded chairs designed by Angèle Parlange.

At left: What was once a blah pass-through space becomes a little exclamation point with bright paint and colorful ceramics in mirror-backed shelves.

The Carleton V trellis wallpaper gives the room dimension and pizzazz. It's also appropriately garden-y. In the room's first iteration, I used furniture I had on hand. A huge sofa slip-covered in green and white stripe, oversized rush-seated arm chairs, large scale contemporary floor lamps, and an industrial strength coffee table. Even the awning came from my old house.

evolve, and we go with that. It's a way of getting unstuck, acknowledging loss, accepting change, and moving forward.

Amen, sister.

Two years later I did not move into Windsor Castle, but I did begin spending time on a ranch in California with the cowboy I met on the blind date at the end of Chapter 12. His house was a large, contemporary design by Hugh Newell Jacobson, if you can imagine anything more different from Bee. I eventually sent my large old friends the chairs and sofa out there, to make us all more comfortable, and the Sofa That Ate Long Island could not eat California, thank heaven, and it fits right in.

When the big sofa and chairs moved out, I rescued from storage Mother's classic low-slung 1960s sofa. It was well made and had held up, but the old Clarence House chintz, pretty as it was, had to go.

Presto, change-o. As it is today, the garden room is furnished a bit more to scale. We refurbished my mother's chic old 1960s sofa and covered it in a Manuel Canovas print. Katharine Hepburn's slipper chairs were also re-upholstered (it was time), and the big round ottoman migrated in from my New York apartment. Curtains add privacy, texture, and warmth. Drawing to left of window is by the late Long Island artist, Robert Dash. It is a prized possession.

88

Think of your rooms in layers that add depth, richness and personal style: from paint, furnishings, and fabrics, to rugs, trims, accessories, and collections.

This Carlton V wallpaper in a trellis pattern pairs well with Benjamin Moore's Powder Sand white and Kiwi green.

I found a great Manuel Canovas linen print to replace it. The two green slipper chairs from the living room were relocated to join the sofa happily. All greens go together. I'm definitely a green person.

Curtains cozy up the room and make it more night-friendly. Something about bare windows at night makes me uneasy—like big black holes that the bogey man might look in.

People are always saying they don't like things to look "decorated" and to look like they've "always been there." Well, safe to say we've got that covered. Hardly anything is new. Lord, sometimes I feel like I live in a flea market.

Notes on Living Areas

Before you do anything to a house, decide how you're going to live in it. A big piece of that is where *you're going to live in it. Plan and furnish accordingly. Is it the living room? The family room? The den? Or the kitchen? Be honest.*

If you don't know what to do with a room, WAIT; it will eventually tell you.

Small rooms seem bigger the more you put in them (to a point); it's all about the arrangement. Pull the furniture into conversation groups away from the walls. Don't shy from big-scale pieces or bold graphics; if it feels fun and right, go for it.

In furniture, aim for a mixture of "legs and skirts." Wood or metal chairs and tables with legs should balance pieces that are upholstered or covered to the floor, like club chairs, sofas, or skirted tables.

Create a dynamic to keep the eye moving around the room. Create contrast with color, tone, texture, art, and objects. Experiment and don't be afraid to change. Vary the heights of tables and chairs.

Painting window mullions a darker color diminishes the boundary between inside and out. Painting interior doors to match the mullions is a unifying element throughout.

High-gloss paint enhances the light and adds subtle pizzazz. So what if the walls aren't perfect?

If ceilings are low, encourage the eye to look up. Install curtain rods to the ceiling. Hang tall mirrors. Use high-back chairs. Group art from wainscoting to ceiling.

Trim lampshades with grosgrain ribbon and augment curtains with contrasting panels of fabric or trim. The layering of details creates depth and a sense of luxury.

Repurpose the dated or out of whack: e.g., we made floor lamps from massive bronze chenets I'd inherited from my mother.

Chapter 19

Tom Samet to the Rescue

Several months into the project, I was overwhelmed. Going in circles, sparring with despair, and despair was winning. I couldn't make headway, and I didn't ask for help. The worst thing is I didn't even think of asking for help. Maybe I thought I didn't deserve help. *You got yourself into this, sister, and you can just figure it out.* I didn't even know what help I needed. Help moving forward from a painful decision with hurtful consequences for people I cared about? Help digging out of boxes and getting organized? Help from a handyman? The answer, of course, was all of the above, and there was one person in particular who was the answer to an unspoken prayer.

Tom's kindness and generosity in those early days were a light in my darkness and a salve to the emotional scrapes and bruises I was so good at hiding.

Decorator and friend Tom Samet, with his avowed affinity for old houses, agreed to help see Bee through, conjuring the kinds of thoughtful and ingenious suggestions I cannot now imagine living without. Like extra shelves in the bathroom. Like (finally) acquiring a proper set of dining chairs. They say the devil is in the details, but Tom took that devil's place, and it has made all the difference. Glazing the living room walls and adding extra panels of contrasting fabric to curtains were his ideas. So were purple lampshades, but we won't talk about that.

Tom also has a darlin' mama (named Frances!), whom he adores. He understood the affection I'd felt for my own mother and my desire to honor her memory by incorporating some of her things into my house. He has been a godsend, truly, and my gratitude is beyond words. Tom's kindness and generosity in those early days were a light in my darkness

and a salve to the emotional scrapes and bruises I was so good at hiding.

Looking back I'm stunned to see how harsh I was with myself. Acknowledging my own vulnerability and weakness, and admitting it to the world by asking for help, is something I now see as courageous. It was also a step toward compassion and forgiveness toward myself, and toward healing.

Chapter 20

The Dining Room and Library

The dining room was a dilemma. It needed to multi-task, but I wasn't sure how. My original thought was to have it double as library and office. But *enh*, it's a public room and a thoroughfare, and I didn't want to look at desk mess every time I walked by. The upstairs study and spare guest room (Chapter 23) would serve as my writing place, and the butler's pantry (Chapter 21) could do home-office duty. But I do have tons of books, and the dining room was the best option for a library. The larger point, though, in the spirit of preserving the formal dining room—which I'm all for—is to let it relax a little into a space that works with the way you actually live. Mine became open storage space, a library, and a repository for collec-

Crown molding and wainscoting enhance a room's dimension and scale. So does using a different color or wall treatment above and below the chair rail.

tions. More recently it has also become an art studio, since we can eat outside in the summer. So much for not looking at a mess, but it's an art-y mess.

Appropriately then, shelving was important. One wall had a 3-by-4-foot niche of glass shelves lit from above, which I love. As for others, those sturdy old French metal and wood étagères were a design inspiration for the garden-shed-meets-manor-house vision I had for Bee. They have a utilitarian elegance that is un-pretentious, yet chic and timeless. These are good replicas—designed by Suzanne Kasler for Hickory Chair Furniture Co.—a splurge, but worth it.

The cases come in two parts, with four top shelves atop two deeper bottom shelves. Since

BEFORE

Before, the dining room was traditionally furnished and arranged, with the table in the center of the room.

Right, the dining room today, with table slightly off center to allow wider passage when not in use. Vintage birdcage painted white and wired for light is swagged to hang over table but can be un-hooked to hang in center of room when table is moved for dinner parties. The Old World Weavers cloth is repurposed from Tom Samet's old curtains. Chairs from Sylvester & Co. in Amagansett.

Turn a random object into a light fixture. The dining room's bird cage fit the bill perfectly, and you won't find it in any catalog.

Double-decker French bakers' shelves by Suzanne Kasler for Hickory Chair were separated to create an ad-hoc sideboard here, with the top halves serving as bookcases, opposite. My kooky collection of pressed botanicals is hung on every wall.

they were too tall for my seven-and-a-half-foot ceilings, I put the bottoms along one wall as serving and storage pieces and put the uppers on either side of the window as bookcases. This is around the time designer and friend Tom Samet (Chapter 19) entered the picture, thank heaven. And with his Yankee directness that invariably tickles my Southern sensibilities, Tom declared that my arrangement looked "like a storeroom," as though a man in a forklift would drive by any minute. He was right, so one of the bottom pieces went to the garden room (Chapter 18).

The house in general reflects an aesthetic of "refined rusticity," and nowhere more so than in the dining room. Traditional architectural elements, Louis LXI-style chairs, and "good" china and silver co-exist peaceably with lowly framed botanicals, stacks of plates, and a jumble of books, sea shells, rocks, birds' nests, and other random objects. It's always changing.

Rooms shouldn't be static, and one of the ways to keep them lively is to change the art and objects displayed in them, however simple or modest.

Tom decreed a pale honey-colored grass cloth above the chair rail and a ragged paint finish below in a slightly lighter shade, adding subtle layers of texture and warmth. He also supplied the Old World Weavers fern-printed burlap tablecloth, fashioned from his own old curtains, like Scarlett o'Hara's dress.

He was skeptical of my idea to off-center the table, but I converted him. It makes the room look larger, and it creates a wider passage from front door to kitchen. It also allows more space for a makeshift art studio set up in front of the window. The huge mirror opposite the window plays with scale and creates the illusion of another window. I don't know if my friend Vicente Wolf started that prop-a-giant-mirror-on-the-floor thing, but

Lately (above) I've come to use the dining room and library as a mini-studio. The north light is nice and I can see children riding their bicycles up and down the street out front. Sometimes tourists stop to take pictures, awww.

Sam's "studio." Top portions of bakers' shelves serve as bookcases.

99

When I think of it, it's a room that reflects my many loves: books, nature, food, the company of friends, and now my Sunday painting, too.

that's who I got it from. I've wanted to lean a mirror on a wall since about 1987, and this was my chance.

The chandelier is an old flea market bird cage I've toted around—birdless—for years and for which I finally found a use. I painted it white and Tom said to fill the bottom with shells. Hung, the birdcage casts the prettiest pattern of light on the ceiling—a delightful surprise.

Botanicals are hung floor to ceiling. I love them and collect them. Shells, too, piled on the lighted glass shelves, are dramatic at night. When I think of it, it's a room that reflects my many loves: books, nature, food, the company of friends, and now my Sunday painting, too. It makes me happy just to pass through this room. To tell you the truth, the whole house is like that.

Set for a party. The shell centerpiece has an elaborate effect but is simple to do. Groups of objects are an interesting alternative to traditional flowers. China, Mottahedeh Torquay.

Notes on Dining and Other Multi-Tasking Rooms

I pray: Lead us not into temptation to abandon the dining room, even if it is seldom used as such. It is so lovely to have when you need it and so easily does double-duty as a library or study, depending on its location.

Don't be afraid of using big pieces in small rooms; they enhance the sense of spaciousness and scale. Big mirrors are especially effective in a small house, and I love them opposite windows. Propping them on the floor evokes vintage and wonderful Vicente Wolf.

Hang your paintings salon-style, floor to ceiling, whether you have limited wall space (which I do) or not. It has a certain eccentric Euro charm, non?

Who says the table has to be smack in the middle of the room? Just make sure the overall furniture arrangement is balanced. Trust your eye.

If your light fixture wiring is centered but your table isn't (see above), attach a hook to the ceiling centered above the table and have enough chain for your fixture to swag it from the center and hang from the hook above the table. If you decide at any time you want to center the table and chairs, maybe when you're entertaining, simply move the table and un-hook the chain, allowing the chandelier to hang in the middle.

Is there a space—doesn't even have to be a room—that you walk through every day that's just blah? Well, you can change that. Hang the Picasso there—or your daughter's rendition thereof. Put in shelves to display a collection, or start a collage or a bulletin board. It's an opportunity for inspiration; seize it!

Wainscoting gives a small room presence. Different treatments above and below it add another layer of interest and texture to the room. You can combine wallpaper and paint, two different textures or paint colors, or different shades of the same hue.

I've pretty much concluded if you have a house anywhere near the beach you can throw shells around pretty much anything and make it look better. Even if you want to avoid cliché (and you do), shells don't count because they are sort of neutral, like gravel or moss.

Chapter 21

The Kitchen
and Butler's Pantry

The kitchen and butler's pantry were the only areas in the house where I started from scratch. A mixed blessing. Too many choices can be as daunting as too few are confining.

The kitchen was straightforward enough. It was a long, narrow galley that had been tacked on to the side of the house in the sixties (I'm guessing). I entertain fairly often and have never minded a galley kitchen. They are efficient, and if you have company while you're cooking, they have no choice but to roost at one end or the other and therefore out of your way. (In theory, anyway.) Arranging it was just a matter of getting that Bermuda Triangle of stove-sink-fridge right. I put the stove across from the sink and the fridge next to the stove, nearest the butler's pantry door, which I figured would be the likeliest point of entry for hungry or thirsty intruders. Heaven help anyone who crosses into the Triangle while I'm cooking.

The kitchen finishes were inspired by a long-coveted kitchen from a house I wrote about for *House Beautiful* a few years ago designed by Abby Rizor and Hattie Wolfe. (Thank you again, Abby and Hattie!) Minding the budget, I chose semi-custom cabinets, which are standard-size cabinets in custom configurations. Ordering them in "paint grade" was less expensive than wood finishes, and to me the painted finishes were more old-fashioned and

A nook in the back corner is dressed up by a collection of blue and white plates and an inherited antique gate leg table that I painted white. Swedish chairs from Tom Samet. Hanging metal chalkboard from General Home Store, East Hampton.

The long, narrow galley kitchen is installed in what was once likely a porch.

better suited to the house. I wanted the color of limed oak, and Benjamin Moore obliged with Manchester Tan. The countertops and drawer pulls were as close to the Rizor-Wolfe inspiration as I could find.

To make it look less kitchen-y, we used only a few upper cabinets and left space for a table and chairs. The exterior wall is blessed with four windows that look out on the herb garden, which is great. The bit of wall near the door got open shelves, where sits my sand collection, among other bits and bobs. My mother's 18th century Irish mahogany table I had previously painted a high-gloss cream color, and designer Tom Samet found the Swedish chairs and plate rack, which we painted gray like the doors and window mullions. No one ever sits there, but it looks good and the table is useful. The big metal chalk "board" was another inspiration for the look of the room,

Opposite: As it is today. Walls are Benjamin Moore Palladian Blue and ceiling is BM Powder Sand, both in high gloss. Counters are Caesarstone. Rug from Madeline Weinrib, ABC Carpet.

Open shelving holds my highly prestigious (but only to me) collection of sand. At Tom Samet's suggestion, a harlequin pattern is stenciled on the shelves, one of those nice details he is so good at.

and I use it to write the evening's menu if I'm entertaining, or for just pure silliness: "Bee Cottage . . . Sweet as Honey," stuff like that.

The mahogany table has recently been moved to the city apartment, replaced with an old painted French *comptoir*, or counter, with wonderful barley twist legs. I bought it years ago in Paris and have finally found a home for it.

Tom suggested the quilted aluminum backsplash for the stove. I would never have

thought of that. The floor, which looks like limed oak, is ceramic tile, which Tom found, and it is genius. My contractor suggested heating the floor from beneath, also genius. The up-front cost is a bit more, but it is very efficient. It feels good, too.

I've always liked the texture and warmth of baskets and pots hanging around. It is very Eighties, I know, but I use them and it's good to have them handy. It also frees up masses of cabinet space.

A metal rod across the windows takes the place of curtains and provides handy storage for baskets and drying herbs.

The Butler's Pantry

Where I grew up in the South, many of the old houses had butler's pantries. By the time I came along, there were more butler's pantries than butlers.

What I came to call the butler's pantry was the house's original kitchen, but over time it had become a sort of ad hoc laundry room—washer here, dryer there, with charming 1920s (or so) glass-front cabinets and a built-in pull-down ironing board in-between. Although we were able to salvage a few of the original cabinets, everything else had to go. (1964 Kenmore range, anyone?) It pained me to lose the little pull-down ironing board, even though I loathe the act of ironing.

The house's original kitchen had morphed into an ersatz butler's pantry and laundry room.

Then once the space was gutted, it languished. I was flummoxed. On the one hand, it was a great design opportunity. And on the other, it was a great design opportunity—if you know what I mean. The pressure! To make things worse, Tom Samet kept telling me it should be "very special," which made me "very nervous." But he was right. It's a major pass-through area and needed to be interesting. Here's what else it needed: shelves for some of my 72 million cookbooks, some kind of desk and office area, storage for china and table linens, a sink, a place to fix flowers, storage for flower-fixing stuff, a bar, and counter space. Piece of cake, right?

Patience. I firmly believe if you let it all swim around in your un-conscious for a while, the

answer will eventually surface. In the meantime, it will drive you crazy.

The solutions seem so obvious now that I can't remember why I was confused about it. (But then I can't remember anything.) Sure enough, one day, bingo: Knee-hole desk and bookshelves on one side with a lower countertop, file drawers, and printer on a pullout shelf in the cabinet. Cabinets and drawers opposite, with a higher countertop and under-counter wine fridge. At the end under the window, a deep sink with a high spigot. A cabinet to one side for flower arranging stuff. Another cabinet on the other side for liquor and drinks. The glasses in the cabinets above. Cabinets are painted in the same manner as the kitchen's cabinets are painted, but the countertops are teak, which will become wonderfully scratched and marred and water-marked over time. My idea of cork tiles between the counter and the cabinets to become the most fun-to-look-at bulletin board ever has a ways to go. Painting the ceiling a glossy turquoise blue seemed like a good use for leftover guest room paint (Chapter 25). The light fixtures are original, with their metal bases painted black.

Now if I could just find that butler . . .

A photo from my Instagram, the afternoon light filtering through the butler's pantry window is a gift everyday.

Now a proper butler's pantry with a desk in the bargain. The higher counter at left is a convenient serving height, also allowing for ample drawers beneath to store linens, flatware, and candles. At right is a desk area with bookshelves above for cookbooks. Countertops are teak. The wall between desktop and bookshelves is corkboard for pinning invitations, photos, and amusing thank-you notes. Light fixtures are original and given a coat of matte black paint. The shimmery blue ceiling—BM Galapagos Turquoise—lends a bit of drama and dash. (In truth it was a good use for paint left over from the guest room upstairs.) Floor is wood-grained ceramic tile, heated from beneath.

Notes on Kitchens and Other Multi-Tasking Rooms

Fool-proof kitchen design: Take stock of all your kitchenware and whatever else you'll need to store in your kitchen (mops, brooms, cleaning supplies?). Map out where everything will go according to how often you use it and how accessible it needs to be, and configure cabinets and drawers accordingly. Maximize storage space by building cabinets up to the ceiling. Glass fronts let you see what's inside.

If your kitchen has limited space, you can almost always find a way to install a bar or a rack for hanging pots, baskets, colanders, and so on. This frees up a lot of cabinet space.

Install pull-out shelves in your lower cabinets. It will be life-changing.

Consider deep drawers in lieu of cabinets. They are very handy. In fact, drawers are handy, period. Make sure you have enough.

Interior cabinet lighting is atmospheric and great if you want to display the contents. But if you light from above and have wood shelves, only the top shelf will be lit. Otherwise the shelves need to be transparent—glass or Lucite. (I goofed, and only the top shelves in the butler's pantry are lit. Not what I wanted. You'd think the contractor would have pointed this out, but no.)

It's nice to have hand soap and hand cream by the sink. I like L'Occitane products for quality and packaging.

Use a kitchen towel and quit using so many paper towels, dammit!

In choosing countertops, do a mess test on a sample to see how much the counter "shows." Do drops of liquid leave a mark? Do a few sprinkles of flour stand up and salute? If so, can the surface be sealed? Is there a comparable color or surface that's more user-friendly? How much wiping do you want to do?

Sorry, GE, but I HATE my refrigerator. Seduced by the look of the double door front, I never bothered to check how it actually opened and closed. One side closes like a normal fridge door; the other you have to close with the New York Giants offensive line. I frequently forget to call in the offensive line. It beeps to signal the door is ajar. I want to shoot it with an AK-47. And then have the Giants stomp it to pieces. Lesson: Research and/or test your appliances as best you can before you bring them home.

While I'm on the appliances subject, status brands are the emperor's new clothes of kitchens. How many bells and whistles do you really need to make ice cubes and fry bacon? If you're on a budget, this is a good place to save. And don't get a double-door fridge until they make one that closes properly.

Inexpensive plastic dividers substitute for fancy built-ins.

Unlike fixed shelves, drawers allow easy storage on the entire surface area, all the way to the back.

Drawers make for easy-to-access storage. I keep this photo taped to the inside cabinet door so guests and staff know exactly how it goes. (And they still don't do it.)

Every little bit counts. Pot lids and roasting pans are kept in the small cabinet above the stove.

Chapter 22

The Master Bedroom

The bedroom. Perhaps the most personal room in the house, and the place where one might feel most loved—or most lonely. At the outset of Bee and me, this room was the most blatant reminder of my recent romantic demise. There I was, just me and my pillows, and the Homer & Jethro country song in my head, "I've Got Tears in My Ears From Lying on My Back in My Bed While I Cry Over You." Actually when I did think of that silly song it made me chuckle . . . a little. Relationship status aside, I do consider the bedroom a haven. The bed is for lullabies and love, not *Seinfeld* reruns.

At 13 x 14, the bedroom is not huge, but it holds a king bed, two side tables, a dresser, an armoire, a bench, two chairs, and five lamps, which is kind of amazing. The bad news is 7 ½-foot ceilings. I can stand flat-footed and touch the ceiling. I am 5'10", but still. Another challenge is a part of the ceiling sloping down under the eaves exactly where the bed goes. "Awkward," as my niece would say. I keep telling myself these quirks are part of Bee's charm.

The way to deal with low ceilings is to lead the eye up. The way to deal with an irregular ceiling or wall is to incorporate it into your design or to ignore it. I incorporated it and

The master bedroom's wonky ceiling begged a wonky treatment. Draping a half-canopy at an angle was an easy solution. The bench at the foot of the bed I bought at auction from Katharine Hepburn's estate. Bedside tables from Mecox Gardens. Madeline Weinrib rug.

BEFORE

BEFORE

then ignored it. A half-canopy camouflages the awkward wall contour, creating height and a dash of drama. I also like the feeling of a small canopy that is open and yet also cozy and sheltering.

Window valances bring the eye up as well. Normally I'd put them clear to the ceiling, but the walls cutting in on either side above one window would have required the valance shape to follow, and would have looked, I daresay, awkward. More charming quirks.

For storage, a single closet and dresser do not quite cover it, so I brought in an armoire I'd had in the city. I still cringe when I think about getting it up the stairs, but here it is, and it does the trick. One quick note: As the armoire was old and the key long lost, its doors would only stay shut with a piece of folded cardboard wedged into them. Tom Samet had a handyman create a magnetic closure with a key permanently installed into the old lock, and it works like an absolute charm. A major convenience from a

Above, two views of the master bedroom before, awkward angles and all.
Opposite, this vintage tufted chair came from the Paris flea market and is the perfect perch for
morning meditation. Lamp from Ruby Beets in Sag Harbor. Antique armoire behind.
Far right, this little niche is directly above the living room fireplace, so it may at one time have been
a working fireplace, too. Now fitted with a shelf and mirror, it makes a sweet dressing table.

Nothing is more welcoming or thoughtful than fresh flowers in a bedroom, even if just a single bloom. "Vases" may come in many forms, such as the odd antique aperitif glass.

A collage of cutouts from old calendar illustrations was a lazy girl's DIY: Images are attached with tiny bits of tape. No fuss, no muss. The glass holds it all in place.

small adjustment. It's the little things in life, right?

The bench at the foot of the bed came from the Katharine Hepburn estate. I bought it at auction along with the two slipper chairs originally in the living room and now in the garden room. I always admired Hepburn's elegance and independence, as well as her indomitable spirit. Having things that once belonged to her is inspiring to me.

The Carleton V floral print and Michael Devine geometric are favorite fabrics and were recycled from the first East Hampton house, which Atlanta designer and long-time friend John Oetgen helped me with. The walls are semi-gloss Wedgewood Gray (Benjamin Moore), a gray-blue plucked from the Carlton V linen. Designer Tom Samet swears men like blue bedrooms, and in a hopeful moment of what-do-I-have-to-lose, I complied.

A small tufted chair with a lamp and garden seat next to it is my "quiet place," where I sit every morning to meditate, pray, and sometimes read. An arched niche in the room was probably once a fireplace, now long covered up. In its place, a shelf and mirror form a sort of dressing table. I cut up illustrations of birds and nests and things from an old calendar and made a collage under the glass on the table. I love it. These small projects that bring such pleasure were a salve to my then-troubled soul. Creating even small bits of beauty calms me and makes me happy, especially when I am down. Makes me think there are at least some things I don't make a mess of.

Nobody wants to admit they feel sorry for themselves, but sometimes we just do. Doing something you are good at helps get you out of it, boosts confidence, and in turn helps you get to the next place you need to be. That's what doing this house did for me.

The Master Bath

I use the term "master bath" loosely, because it is really the central bath in the house. Located at the top of the stairs with its door opening directly onto the hall landing, the ideal would be to try to make it look more like a room than a bathroom, and decoratively to continue the theme of the bedroom "suite." In order to accomplish that, we put an arched wooden cornice above the tub and made a floor-length curtain in the same Michael Devine fabric as the bedroom canopy. Try as I might to keep the door closed, it just doesn't always happen, so now at least you see the pretty curtain, though the tile floor does sort of give away that a loo might be lurking nearby. But having it even slightly less obvious is somehow a little nicer.

Shelves above the loo in the master bath hold a collection of "smalls," paintings and figurines, with bits of moss for color and contrast.

Chapter 23

The Study and Sometimes Guest Room

I need a dedicated place to write and work. Why was I so reluctant to acknowledge that? Is it because part of me subconsciously believed that writing and art are not valued as highly as "real" work like doctoring, lawyering, or banking, and so how could it deserve its own room? I was neurotically reluctant to commandeer a spare bedroom for my ("frivolous") work, but eventually, I did just that (selfishly!). As I sit in this very room writing this, and knowing how much work I've done here, I laugh today at the thought of feeling I needed to justify myself to myself in my own house for heaven's sake. I also smile at the analogy. Claiming space for my work was a small act of self-validation, if not entirely banishing a bit of my spurious subconscious, then surely chipping away at it. If you can't knock off the whole block at once, then chip away. Eventually it will crumble.

As neither dining room/library nor butler's pantry/office offered even a modicum of privacy, the only other choice for my writing space was the spare bedroom upstairs. I love having houseguests, but the truth is I spend more time here writing and working on creative projects than needing an overflow guest room. So I'll repeat myself: decide how you are going to live in a place before you decorate it—my number one design rule.

It's nice to have a desk by a window, but if that's not possible, the effect of a window can be created with a grid of framed paintings, in this case pages from my travel sketchbooks. My writing desk is an old laminate dining table with a burlap cover. Kooky antique Venetian lamp. Chairs from Sylvester & Co. are borrowed from dining room.

A daybed is a good solution for a room that multi-tasks as a study and occasional guest room.

BEFORE

Above: In its former life, a bedroom . . .

Opposite: How I fit all this in here I do not know, but it works. Antique French daybed is great for reading, napping, and extra guests. Antique wing chair remains in the muslin it came in, but we covered the cushion in a Manuel Canovas check. Small slipper chair in Scalamandré velvet from two houses ago. Pastel above bed is by Wolf Khan.

The master and spare of Bee's bedrooms are at the front of the house. The third bedroom at the back is the official guest room. Most of the time I really only need one guest room.

The plan was that if I could figure how to get a desk, a daybed (for naps and for overflow guests), a dresser, and a chair or two in the spare bedroom, then the spare bedroom could also work as my study. Of course there is a radiator right where the desk should go, along with other, ahem, charming architectural quirks. One corner of the room, where the door is, is catty-cornered. So there would be nothing to do but arrange around it. And as with the master bedroom, the 7 ½-foot ceilings slope under the eaves. Once again the answer is to make the eye go up. High-backed wing chairs, obelisk étagères, and tall desk lamp lend verticality. I ignore the sloping eaves. I can hear my mother, "Don't call attention to it, and no one else will either." I just hope people don't bump their heads.

After trying every conceivable arrangement, it all fits, and if I do say so myself, it is a triumph. It is a triumph, however, only possible with "Magic Sliders." Those stick-on silicone discs are genius. You attach them to the bottoms of furniture legs, and you can, as it says on the package, *move everything as if on wheels! As seen on TV!* I have them on everything; otherwise I would be in traction.

To further expand the space and enhance the light, a large mirror is hung above the dresser, giving the effect of another window as it reflects the one across from it. I love a mirror hung opposite a window. The huge gilded frame reaches nearly to the ceiling, and I am the first to say it is faintly ridiculous here—as it would belong better above a grand sideboard in some Georgian manor house or similar. Well, I say to the mirror, love the one you're with. And why be predictable?

As this room and the master are adjacent, and as both rooms are visible from the stair landing, I felt they should be treated decoratively as a suite. The palette is predominantly blue, gray, and white, with the study getting a shot of yellowy-green picked up from a Wolf Khan landscape and repeated in a painted dresser. The high gloss Palladian Blue (Benjamin Moore) goes from the stairway and hall into the study.

I had wanted to put the desk under the window, but there was the radiator. So I created the idea of a window by hanging sixteen identically framed watercolors

Stake Your Claim

Okay, so here's a thought.

Take a minute to think about what it is you love doing but deny yourself because you think it has no value or is not "productive" somehow. Listen, if you love it, then it's in your heart. If it's in your heart, then it's in your soul and it's part of your purpose. Following your heart means leading the life you were meant to live, and that might mean letting go of the life you thought you were supposed to live (to paraphrase Joseph Campbell). That might mean recognizing you need a room of your own, an hour of your own, a garden, a dog, an easel, a food processor. Whatever it means to you today, tomorrow, five years from now, listen to that.

Every one of us has a saboteur lurking within; recognizing it is the first step to defeating it, or at least to using it to our advantage. When we design our houses in a way that supports and validates who we are and what we do, there is less room for the saboteur to assert itself and more room for your true self to shine.

in a grid, like windowpanes, above the desk. The pieces are framed pages from my travel sketchbooks and of interest likely to no one but me, but they are treasured mementoes, and there is a story in every one.

Incorporating into your décor these small reminders of your and your family's fond memories is a way our homes can be made to inspire and encourage us. Another example in this same room is the desk. It is my mother's old breakfast table, and using it as my writing table is a tribute not just to her but to family, and history, and, well, just to making what you have work. But most of all I like to think her spirit is there with me, cheering me on and supervising my syntax. Originally a bright green laminated Parson's table, the desk's size and scale were good but the color wrong. A burlap tablecloth solves the problem and provides storage hidden beneath. An opening in the cloth's center inverted pleat allows easy access and has a Velcro closure. A covered box holds cards and stationery; otherwise I keep here only what I need in order to write. There is a tray with pencils, pens, pads, and paperclips, and a

The sketchbook pages are framed with spacers between the mat and the paper, so they appear to float. I hang most of my own art, but hired a pro to execute this grid, which would have driven me crazy.

few objects that are nice to look at when I get the stare-ies, which I sometimes do when I'm meant to be writing.

The more functions you want a room to provide, the more challenging it is to arrange and furnish. This study-and-sometimes-guest-room took time to sort out, and now that it's sorted, I can't imagine it any other way. It was an object lesson in taking one's own advice to let a problem area simmer while you work in other areas you're confident about. In Bee's case, probably the easiest area of all was the "real" guest room, or so-called guest suite, down the hall.

A bronze doré and enamel candelabrum of my mother's I had made into a little lamp. Vintage flea market watercolor with bee trinket. / Opposite: This large gilded mirror is a bit unexpected, but I love how it reflects the light of the window opposite. Painted chest came from my old house in Tarboro.

Notes on Furniture Arranging, Repurposing, and Making Things Work

----

Rooms can be puzzles. If you have a lot of pieces that don't "fit," just let them float around in there and don't think about it for a while. Sometimes you'll return and see a piece that fits, and it all comes together. You'd be surprised.

If it is a multi-tasking home-office/bedroom space, keep linens and pillows in a nearby closet for easy access. And be sure there is a chair, a light, and some sort of nightstand or table beside the bed.

Be open to using furniture or objects in unexpected ways. For example, a mirror you might normally picture in a living or dining room might work in a home office. A sofa or loveseat in a dining room might work. A stove in a bedroom . . . nah. But you see what I mean.

If a piece of art is not working for you or for the room, consider changing the frame. The Wolf Khan drawing I loved had a big gold frame that I didn't love. Reframing it made all the difference, and now the drawing shines instead of the frame.

Skirted tables are great for storage, but organize the stuff so it is easily accessible and pin a discreet little list on or near the table to remind you what's under there.

Chapter 24

The Guest Suite

As mentioned, I'd planned to begin my second marriage in this house. That didn't happen, sadly, and my fiancé's sons, for whom the guest room was substantially destined, never did stay here either. But at the very beginning of the renovations I was still expecting them, so I had them in mind when I started. Funnily enough it is the one area I had total clarity on from the start. I had—and have—deep affection for those young men, and G was a good father. We had fun together. In retrospect I wonder if there is a parallel between the clarity of my feeling for G's boys and the confidence with which I decorated "their" room. In that vein, I wonder if there might be clues in our rooms that echo other issues in our lives?

A quasi-nautical theme appealed in an obvious way because the house is near the ocean, but also because of the room's diminutive size. It is small for a house but big for a boat, so instead of a small guest room, it is large stateroom. Other optimistically interpreted architectural attributes of the 9-by-12-foot room with 7-foot ceilings is that it is cozily (to say the least) tucked under the eaves, making it almost A-framed.

One good thing about it is that is has two windows, one of which overlooks the garden. Another is its privacy. From the upstairs landing, a door opens to a small corridor leading to a bathroom, linen closet, built-in set of drawers, and the bedroom. So it is a self-contained suite and works well both practically and decoratively.

The tiny guest room is cozy, colorful, and comfortable. Custom Leontine Linens give the room personality. The bee appliqué is taken after the cutout in the garden gate. Staffordshire dogs repurposed into lamps. Vintage turquoise glass pitcher.

I chose a dark, high-gloss turquoise-y blue (Benjamin Moore Galapagos Turquoise) to envelop the bedroom, ceiling included. It reminds me of the ocean, waves and all, thanks to the bumpy old stucco walls. It is counter-intuitive, but dark colors in small spaces minimize shadows, and that visually expands the space. Designer and friend Richard Keith Langham told me that a dark color on the ceiling makes it disappear into the night, and he is right.

Designer Tom Samet told me to do two things that were so spot-on, they made the rest of the room fall easily into place. One was to order the woven twin beds from Pottery Barn (since discontinued). The second

BEFORE

Left: Measuring about 9 x 12, the guest room, before.

Far left: Still measuring about 9 x 12, the guest room, after. A small space painted a dark color appears larger because the shadows are less visible, causing the walls visually to recede. (Sounds good to me anyway.) Walls and ceiling in high gloss Benjamin Moore Galapagos Turquoise. The bed legs have stick-on silicone sliders ("Magic Sliders") making them easy to move.

Above: Window treatments are simple roller shades. Beach-y embroidered pillows from Calypso Home nestle in the window seat.

BEFORE

was to paint the built-in drawers in the corridor dark brown, which makes them look like a piece of furniture. The dark chocolate also in the bedroom is a crisp contrast to the white of the sheets and woodwork. Another Tom detail is a piece of glass atop the radiator cover, making it look finished and more furniture-like.

Once-vivid-now-faded cranberry lampshades and bolster pillows add a nice pop, rounding out the nautical red, white, and blue without saying "red, white, and blue," if you know what I mean. In truth the cranberry comes in because by dern I was going to use the pair of red and white embroidered star and crab pillows (I already owned) if it killed me. And look where they end up, adrift in the window seat, an afterthought. But I like them nonetheless, and I thank them for their inspiration.

You may notice around the house a surfeit of Staffordshire figurines. Most are inherited from my mother. She loved them and so do I. Tom suggested we make lamps of a pair of dogs. Unprompted I would probably not have done that for this room, but it works in a WASP-y, Bunny Williams sort of way, and I mean that as a compliment both to WASPs and to Bunny. Window treatments amount to simple, white roller shades.

Before: A narrow hall connects the landing at the top of the stair to the "guest wing" comprising bedroom, bathroom, linen closet, and built-in drawers. The proximity of the bed to the door gives you an idea of the size of the room.

Today: The built-in drawers at right are given a shiny coat of Benjamin Moore Tudor Brown, making them look like furniture. Leaning against the wall at left is an old fish-drying rack, painted the same brown and used as a magazine rack. The bit of blue peeking out at the end brightens the whole space.

Notes on Guest Rooms and Guests

A while back, Shannon Ables of the Simply Luxurious blog asked me to write a guest post for her on guest rooms, so she gets credit for this chapter. Thanks Shannon!

In my early married (first-time) days in my twenties, when we went to a wedding every fifteen minutes, we went to one in Birmingham, Alabama. I'd never been, but honey that Mountain Brook area is something. Our elegant hosts brought us breakfast in bed. That was pretty dang fab.

The likelihood of that happening at my house is right up there with my doing the Watusi naked in church. Never say never, but just saying.

Bee Cottage is busiest in the summer, when summer travelers means summer company. The more desirous your location, the more likely you are to have house-guests. It's funny how that works. Decorating aside, a welcoming, comfortable guest room can be created with the simplest of luxuries, even if the room is tiny. What's involved is more effort than expense, but it is easily accomplished. I find the simple ritual of preparing for company to be very satisfying.

A thoughtfully prepared guest room conveys kind-ness, caring, respect, and even love. When I was away at school and came home for holidays, I wasn't a "guest," but my darlin' Mama always had fresh flowers in my room. Nothing elaborate—a few roses or a single ginger lily. She saw to it that everything was fresh and fluffed up, with the latest magazines by the bed, and sometimes a book or memento of something she'd enjoyed and wanted to pass along. She did this for our houseguests, too, naturally, and I've simply followed behind her.

As for the visit itself, before your guests arrive, give them an idea of the schedule they can expect. If it is a weekend stay, let them know what activities are in-volved and what sort of clothes they'll need. If their ar-rival and departure times need to be confirmed, do so at the beginning. It's nice also to convey a general idea of your and your family's routine. Do you get up early and go to a spin class? Take a morning walk? Do you or your children take a nap or have quiet time in the afternoon? This is all good information for guests to know.

When they arrive, give them time to unpack and settle in before you launch them into the breach. Or the beach.

Before bedtime, let everyone know the morning drill. I keep it simple, organizing coffee cups, juice glasses, plates, napkins etc. the night before and then getting up early to make the coffee and tea, putting out some fruit or berries, and croissants or toast. This way guests may graze at their leisure without me hovering. I also may leave a newspaper or two, sometimes with a note as to my morning schedule or whereabouts if it is before nine. While I am an early riser, I am not an early chatter. Guests are free to ease into the day on their own. Some-times on a weekend it's nice to take the low-mainte-nance route on Saturday and then have a proper break-fast or brunch on Sunday, with everyone sitting around the table re-capping the previous days' hijinks. "Down-loading" a friend of mine calls it. "Gossip," I call it.

The Guest Bath

The good news in the bathroom is that it is large in relative comparison to the bedroom. To save money I kept the existing floor and fixtures. The painted stripes are meant to mimic a beach cabana—unexpected and fun. It's also a distraction from the room's awkward angles and dated fixtures and floor tiles.

An old bamboo bookcase found a home here and is used to store towels and other bath supplies. It also gives guests a surface for cosmetics, jewelry, and whatnot.

I splurged (as I did in the master bedroom and bath) on Leontine bedding and towels, embroidering them with my little signature bee. To me Leontine is the Hermes scarf of linens.

Pops of color are added with vintage linen hand towels and soap.

If you must live with a wacky-shaped bathroom or old tiles and fixtures, consider a bold paint treatment to draw attention from the sore points. Painting the guest bath like a big, striped beach cabana is fresh and fun.

*The guest bath, before: Old
fixtures and black and
white tile were deemed
worth keeping.*

*Today: Painted in a bold
awning stripe but otherwise
untouched, the guest bath
is transformed.
Vintage bamboo étagère
holds towels and extras.*

Chapter 25

The Pergola

Outdoor rooms magically increase a house's living space. Bee Cottage originally had a brick patio off the garden room and a small flagstone terrace off the dining room, with a grapevine-covered(!) pergola. I didn't dare touch that little piece of pretend Provence, but the brick patio had room to grow. Bee is really all about the garden, and sadly there is precious little view of it from inside the house. A large porch looking on to it is the next best thing; and a covered, heated porch is even better. From April to November, this is the most lived-in space of the house.

In planning, I knew it had to have many things: ample seating and dining areas, a place for a grill, and a retaining wall, or "sitting wall" that can be for seating or for a surface on which to put drinks or hors-d'oeuvres. Ina Garten had carried on about hers when I wrote about her East Hampton "barn" for *House Beautiful* some years ago, and who am I to argue with Ina? There also needed to be steps to the kitchen door, which handily could be built into a structure for two storage areas. The small landing also serves as a convenient place to put down your groceries or tote bag while you open the door, talk on your mobile, let the dog out, text your girlfriend, and keep from messing up your pedicure.

Landscape designer Jane Lappin and her able associate Adrienne Woodduck drew up a plan to suit the English cottage-y style of the house, in stucco and stone. What stumped us

The metal furniture and pouf came from designer Richard Keith Langham's tag sale years ago. Sunpak outdoor heaters installed overhead were a gift from my new beau, the fellow I met in Chapter 12.

was how to cover it. A wooden pergola with cascading wisteria? A spiffy canvas awning? What proved ideal was a bit of both: a framed pitched roof with a canvas cover, put up in April and taken down in November. As for furniture, the Richard Keith Langham-designed metal settee and chairs and ginormous pouf I'd bought years ago at his tag sale were just right, and the cushions are the very blue of Bee's gates and shutters. I'm not normally inclined to match like that, but occasionally it's called for. Ditto with the awning and painting the all-weather wicker chairs. Budget-fatigued, I strung outdoor café lights and called it a day. Sometimes the simplest solutions are the best. It's exhausting to try to be clever all the time, not to mention tedious.

Stucco pillars and a low "sitting wall" support a wooden beam roof structure. A canvas awning comes on and off with the seasons.

Opposite, left: The pergola and patio as seen from the kitchen door. Top right: Fluffed up for a party. Pillows from Dransfield and Ross. Below right: Storage areas on either side of the kitchen steps create ample flat surfaces handy for informal buffets.

Chapter 26

The Garden

I like how the British say garden instead of yard. If they have a patch of dirt with one blade of grass on it, it's a garden. It sounds so much nicer than yard, where livestock are fed. As much as I love this house, from the beginning it was about the garden. I'd never had a real one. In the years I'd lived on my own, I'd had only the tiniest gardens, and in New York, none at all. Despite my not having the greenest thumb in the world, I wanted a garden. My mother could stick a coat hanger in the ground and it would grow, I swear. Surely I could learn to manage a smallish but wonderful garden. What's left of one-third of an acre after you put a house, a pool, a terrace, and a driveway—is manageable. We set to work on a plan before the ink was dry on the sales contract.

The East End of Long Island boasts the work of many talented garden designers, but when friend and real estate agent Frank Newbold told me about Jane Lappin, I felt she was the one. Frank relayed how once upon a time Jane had successfully re-interpreted the famous Sissinghurst White Garden for his

Opposite, Bee Garden at about year two. At right, the garden, before.

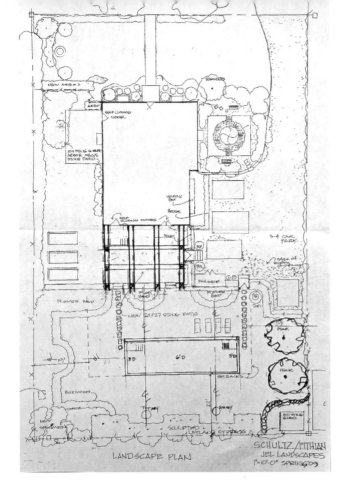

The original landscape plan as devised by Jane Lappin of Wainscott Farms. Like all plans, it evolved over time, but the basic bones are there.

The western exposure, before.

Facing west, today, with ivy topiaries inspired by those at Hidcote.

own little cottage, and that was all I needed to hear. Her roster of high-profile and highfalutin clients was irrelevant at best and intimidating at worst; but once we met, all that fell away. She immediately had a feel for what would be appropriate for the property. I wanted it to be correct, but I wanted to have some fun with it as well. She got that. And frankly, I couldn't afford mistakes.

The back (south) and west side are the formal parts of the garden. "Formal" as in of form, not as in fancy. Hedges really are the bones of the back garden. Though it is a typical cottage-y

Side lawn and grape arbor, before.

Before, the east end of the garden abuts directly to my neighbors' ivy-covered garage, a nice green backdrop.

Today, with raised beds, mostly for herbs.

Same view today, with an armillary made by Gary Hume.

garden, it has the structure of the boxwood hedge to formalize it and keep it from being too loose and blowsy. I am enthralled with the work of the Belgian landscape designer Jacques Wirtz, who knows a thing or two about hedges as architecture. Heaven knows if the Hamptons have anything, they have hedges. (Perry Guillot's brilliant, illustrated *Privet Lives: An Imaginary Tale of Southampton's Iconic Shrub* is a treasure, as is Perry.) I don't have a big high hedge in front like the grand estates do, but I have them in the back (mainly because I don't want anybody who doesn't have to to see me in a bathing suit). Bee's garden had hedges—a little scraggly, but a start. The

south border, we decided, would not be flowery, so we wanted the hedge there to be more interesting, sculptural perhaps, a la Wirtz. Jane came up with the design to have them curve outward, like buttresses. The garden benches came from a mountain house I had years ago. I'm so glad I kept them, but for the life of me, neither I nor Atlanta designer John Oetgen, who brought them for me back in the nineties, can remember where they came from.

The southwest corner with summer beds in all their glory. Hollyhocks, dahlias, hydrangeas, matricaria, azuratum, salvia, delphiniums, and snapdragons bursting out of a low boxwood hedge.

It is a bit extravagant, not to mention high-maintenance, to have so many annuals, but bless their hearts, they just give and give. From May until October, the dahlias bloom their big floppy heads off and you gotta love 'em. And no, we do not dig them up and replant them the next year; we just start all over again. Over the years, for economy's sake, we have begun to replace some of the annuals with roses and other perennials. They, too, give generously.

The raised herb beds seen through rose-colored petunias.

The thing about perennials is that you have two or three weeks of show and they're over. The trick is planting the garden to have something blooming all the time. Then you spend the rest of your life telling visitors they should have seen it last week. I have a great deal to learn, but in the meantime the garden absolutely makes my heart sing.

The erstwhile bird topiaries were originally made as decoration for the wedding reception I did not have. But I loved the topiaries and not using them made me sadder than using them, if that makes sense. So I did. They were stuffed with soil and sprigged with ivy and weighed ten thousand pounds. That turned out to be a less-than-ideal solution. They have since been defoliated and now await their next destiny. I may just keep them in their original wire form and call it a day. Or I might slipcover them in all-weather fabric awning stripes and put them back by the pool. That would be fun.

The big metal urns came from an antiques shop in town that is no longer there, sadly. I had them in the dining room in my first East Hampton house. The plinths give them a bit more importance, enhancing them architecturally without making them pretentious.

The east end of the garden originally had two pear trees, but they just weren't doing it for me. We were thinking about a pergola covered with roses or wisteria in that spot, but I was out of money at that point. So we created another "room" with privet hedges, and I added a dopey swing because I just love a swing.

But no one ever used the swing, so in 2013 I got rid of it and replaced it with a giant, rustic armillary I found at the local summer antiques show. I am a fool for armillaries. I don't know why. The Japanese maples at either side echo the deep red color of the armillary's

When planning a porch or a pool, consider how you'll use it, where you'll sit, where the sun comes in, which way the wind blows, where the grill goes, and what the views are.

rusted iron and give that end of the garden color and contrast. The maples appear to be in planters, but the bottoms have been removed, allowing the trees to be planted directly into the ground.

The herb garden is my play garden. A monkey could grow herbs, so even I cannot mess them up. I also plant lettuces and arugula, and they actually grow, and I think I am Frederic Law Olmsted. The twig tuteurs give a rustic cottage-y touch and a bit of architecture.

The grapevine-covered metal arbor is original to the house and like a little piece of Provence. I thought the grapes would be messy, but they aren't. I use them in arrangements and on the table when entertaining. Remarkably, the horrific Hurricane Sandy of 2012 damaged little else at Bee but the arbor. My neighbor's apple tree fell on it, and it looked like a giant bird with a broken wing. Thanks to my terrific caretaker Diana Harty and handyman Basilio Parada who fixed it, it is as good as old.

The thing about gardens is that they are never finished, ever. They are never perfect. Yet they are so wonderful. That gives me great joy, and great hope.

The Pool

Before August, the North Atlantic is too cold for my Southern bones, so I wanted a warm(ish) pool. They say immersion in water cleanses your energy field, and I get in it nearly every day. Although on some days the blow-dry trumps the energy field.

There was a perfect rectangle of lawn begging for a pool, and designer Jane was happy to oblige. Between the time we spoke and the time we met—she'd been working on the garden design for some weeks by then—I began to think about the particulars of a pool. Since I was just going to use it for laps and quick dips, there was no need for a diving board or deep end, and my Marco-Polo days (thank God) are over. Make it shallow, I thought, the better the sun can warm it. So we decided that the depth should be 4 feet at either end and 6 feet in the middle.

Ah, the perils of long distance landscaping. I arrived at Bee one weekend thrilled to see the hole dug and the re-bar laid . . . in the wrong place, by about ten feet to the left. I fretted over it something terrible, wondering if I could live with it. I couldn't. Ouch. Thank goodness the concrete wasn't poured yet. They say everything happens for a reason, and in retrospect I wonder if the pool gods were trying to tell me to

The west end of the garden accommodates 5 tables of 8 or 10 for dinner, which is about what my kitchen can accommodate. I try to remember this when I find myself wishing the pool were longer.

make a larger pool, which I now wish I had. Mine, at 11-by 38-feet, is a bit short as a lap pool, unless you are 18 inches tall or a very small dog.

In all seriousness, I've become increasingly attuned to the potential significance of so-called accidents. Sure, sometimes a goof is just a goof, but sometimes it is a message. I've come to see wisdom in wondering about a seemingly random event or mishap, and at least to look at it from different perspectives. Almost invariably there is an insight to be had, or a solution to a problem, or a touch of grace.

This does not explain, however, my notion of installing a fountain in the pool. It is nuts-o—there is no other word for it. Well, ridiculous may be a word for it. Also silly and one-hundred-percent impractical. And yet . . . I hoot with laughter every time I turn it on (even when I am by myself, which is a bit worrying). Spouts shooting dainty arcs of water line both long sides of the pool. The settings are adjustable, beginning with a small arc and up to full-on Bellagio style, which is higher than my head and absolutely preposterous.

Interestingly, Jane said the fountain is what ultimately inspired her design and gave the garden the light-hearted, touch-of-whimsy tone that made it sing. Like music, gardens are a tonic for the soul if ever there was one.

Notes on Landscaping and Pools

Definitely, definitely have a master plan for your garden and landscape. It helps you determine priorities and budget accordingly. The landscape frames the house and says as much about its inhabitants as the interiors do. Don't be frustrated if you can't do all you want at first. I don't need to remind you how quickly time flies.

Working with a professional to develop a plan will save you tons of time and probably pay for itself in due course. If you are a novice gardener like me, just be sure to ask questions at every turn about maintenance and care, and be realistic about your budget both for money and time.

That said, once you have the master plan, know that it will change, and allow it to evolve. It bears repeating that gardens are never finished. That is their madness and their joy.

Trim hedges narrower at the top so sunlight can reach bottom branches.

Don't think deer don't eat everything because they do. We put netting over the ivy on the front of the house and over the hollies at the side. It seems to work   for now.

If at all feasible to irrigate window boxes and containers, do so.

Do think about how you are going to use the pool. If you are going to swim laps, take the occasional dip, or even just look at it, it can be quite shallow. A shallow pool is less expensive to build and to maintain because it requires less of everything.

Consider a salt water filtration system. It is so much better for your skin, eyes, and hair.

Remote controls for pool lights and heat are convenient. Though I am usually too cheap to turn on the heat, I like knowing I can.

Chapter 27
Collections

To be honest I never fancied myself a collector, per se, because to me the term implies a refined and conscious pursuit of a particular item of a certain quality. My approach is more haphazard, more a guided accumulation of things that make me smile, or remember fondly, or merely please me. Somehow many of these things have ended up at Bee Cottage, so the question becomes what to do with them. Here is a sampling: baskets; bee things (well duh); bird's nests, houses, and cages; books (I swear they multiply in my sleep); botanicals; china; sand; shells; shoes (but we won't go there); small paintings of land- and seascapes; my own silly sketchbooks; Staffordshire figurines; and stones. All carry memory and sentiment; few claim intrinsic value. What's important about collections in decorating is that they reveal something of the heart of the inhabitant. A collection—whether it's Monets or matchbooks—is by definition personal, and decorating void of personality might as well be a hotel lobby.

Apart from the books, which I've done nothing clever with but stick them in shelves—including in the "dining library" in Chapter 20, the umpteen Staffordshire figurines

Opposite page, clockwise from top left: This brightly painted landing between garden room, living room, and butler's pantry is a little showcase for Sunderland jugs and Staffordshire. / Leave it to me to bring sand to the beach, but well-traveled sand it is, from the beaches of California to the deserts of Africa. / The collage of paintings at my bedside continues to grow. They are lovely to wake up to. / The dining room (also at left) is a cabinet of curiosities, with plant specimens, china, books, birds' nests, elephants' teeth, river rocks, shells, and Lord knows what else.

Above, part of my mother's collection of Stafford-shire figurines. Below, kitchen baskets within easy reach./ Opposite, a few of the bee things collected by me or gifted by friends. Clockwise from top left, an appliquéd pillow, needlepoint coaster, pin tray, slippers, straw skep/antique print/beehive candles, and a tiny bee ornament.

inherited from Mama were the most demanding of accommodation. (I do love them, but thank goodness my sister got half.) Niches in upstairs and downstairs halls took on a few pieces. We built shallow shelves at the foot of the stairs for the rest.

It is an old saw in decorating that the massing of like objects has greater visual impact than those dispersed higgledy-piggledy. It is as true of porcelains as it is of more modest prizes, like sand from places I've traveled to, from the Namib Desert to Nassau. Sand is a great souvenir, and free. I have canisters for some of it, and glass vases for the rest. That they vaguely resemble containers used for flour and sugar may be what prompted me to place them in the kitchen. I just hope no one tries to bake a cake with a cup of St. Bart's beach.

My baskets are not consciously collected. They are more functional than anything else. But because they are so often used, it is nice to have them visible and accessible. They look pretty hanging in the kitchen and don't take up valuable shelf and cabinet space.

Some collections are more theme- than object-oriented. I love birds and gravitate toward birdy

things. Birds and bees go together, after all. And though I do not like the idea of a caged bird, I do like bird cages. I also like birds' nests, eggs, and houses. Note that the groupings rule need not always apply. While the houses can form their own little neighborhood on the porch sitting wall, they can also be scattered about to create a composition or vignette, or just to add an interesting shape.

Why I have such a thing about pressed plants, I do not know. Was I a botanist in another life? The dining room

From the top: Detail of master bathroom shelf. / Houses for birds and butterflies. / Some collections, like China, silver, and linens, are useful.

holds about five collections of these, and there are more in the basement (oy). Hanging them floor to ceiling was a practicality because of the limited wall space; it's also an effective display. I wouldn't do it with a Chagall, but a daffodil is okay.

Upstairs, old sketchbook pages are framed and hung in a grid in the Study (Chapter 23), and another group of small paintings occupy a wall in the master bedroom (Chapter 22).

Sometimes it is fun to arrange items in unexpected places, like a decorative display of plates in the kitchen, or a collection of figurines and other "smalls" on bathroom shelves, a departure from the usual hairspray and Kleenex. Little surprises keep a house from being too serious.

Notes on Collections

Arrange objects by theme, color, texture, shape, or whatever pleases your eye. Balance them by visual "weight" and scale. There are no rules here; play with your groupings and change when you feel like it.

There are no rules either as to where collections are displayed. Kitchens, baths, hallways, and stairwells can always use a little perking up. A house that arouses a bit of amused astonishment is fun.

Hang paintings or decorative plates in groups. Balance your composition by keeping about the same space between each. And nothing says you can't go floor to ceiling or combine paintings, plates, mirrors, brackets, figurines, and sculpture. Trying arrangements on the floor first is always a good idea. If your collection is large and varied, start with the bigger pieces and fill in from there. If you feel overwhelmed by the task, call a professional art installer. If you don't know one, call a local art gallery for a recommendation. It is money well spent.

Painting backs of shelves a bold or deep color shows off their contents and adds contrast and drama, especially for stodgy old books.

Lighting is key. Even the humblest of objects looks sculptural and substantial when well lit. Home stores today offer an array of DIY options for picture lights, spotlights, up-lights, and in-shelf lighting.

You can collect and display just about anything, from the serious (art and antiques) to the silly (Pez dispensers, anyone?). What do you like? What makes you laugh? What evokes fond memories? What do you want your home to say about you? Your collections can speak volumes.

Bee Cottage, August 1, 2014

It is my sixth summer at Bee Cottage. Every day here is special, maybe more so now that there are fewer of them—East Hampton is a long way from California. Um-hmm. Life has changed and boy howdy. I almost can't remember what it was like Before Bee. (Of course, I can't remember what I had for breakfast. Wait, did I have breakfast . . . ?)

Seriously. Tom Dittmer, the handsome fellow I had the blind date with in Chapter 12 is the same one who gave me the porch heaters in Chapter 25, and the same one I'm married to in Chapter Now. We were the bride and groom from AARP. The thing is, Tom lives in California. Or rather we live in California, on a ranch in the Santa Ynez Valley north of Santa Barbara. The landscape couldn't be more different from East Hampton, or more beautiful. No one feels luckier than I do, or more surprised. Hey, and I had children after all—a son and daughter who are both grown and married, two grandsons who are fond of lizards, two granddaughters who are not, and a little baby granddaughter who is as yet undecided regarding lizards.

The mother of Tom's children, also named Frances if you can believe, was also a wonderful part of our lives. She came to our wedding. We spent Thanksgivings together and visited at other times. And now that I think of it, damn if Frannie didn't encourage me to write a memoir. She died earlier this year in a plane crash. I wrote her obituary. There was a lot to say.

California is home now, though we keep a pied-à-terre in Manhattan. I manage about six weeks a summer at Bee, offsetting costs with occasional renters. The bi-coastal thing is a challenge, a "high-class problem" for sure, but one that does require much energy and time. The same goes for maintaining three households. (The ranch runs fine without me, though nicer with me, if I do say so myself.) My margins are narrower now, in everything from energy, to

Tom Dittmer and I were married in 2012, in the olive grove at Rancho la Zaca, our home in California.

time, to money. That's been a while sinking in, and now that it has, I'm thinking something's got to give. When we are pulled in twenty directions, our compass gets confused.

This summer, a relentlessly rainy Fourth of July found me mopping water in Bee's basement that supposedly does not flood—unless it does. A morning of tossing wet, ruined things prompted donating or selling even more. The stuff was perfectly good but merely taking up space. Providentially, I had just read a book called *Everything That Remains: A Memoir by the Minimalists*, by Joshua Fields Millburn and Ryan Nicodemus, and something sparked. I was ready to do some clearing—in the basement and elsewhere.

If we are paying attention, God, nature, or a flooded basement gives a nudge, and we have to act. Awareness in one area of life, even the basement (maybe especially the basement)—can lead to awareness in another. What's in the basement of my head? My heart? My life? Is it adding value? Is it helping me to add value to others?

Maybe it is not so much perfect bliss we seek, but rather self-awareness. The Buddhist principle of detachment from self-imposed suffering is in its essence the ability to recognize our own neurotic patterns and step aside from them. We aren't necessarily "cured" of them; we just aren't caught up in them. The openness and effort to learn sustains our momentum to grow and change. It gives us the confidence to admit that things, thoughts, people, or places that worked for us at one time in life may not work in another. Letting go creates the space in our closet/day/life for the new/better/right to come in—or maybe there is just space, and that's great, too. There is no magic pill for a muddle-free existence, but there may be a way to keep one muddle from spilling into another.

The answer for me, in a word, is Authenticity. Your own word may be different, but your desire the same. By being true to who we are, we know who we can be. Being authentic allows us to see our soul's blueprint, intuit our purpose, fulfill our mission, and make our hearts sing.

Anything else is clutter.

So the journey continues with another series of choices—not in paint colors and curtains, but in priorities, in recognizing what's important, in winnowing away what no longer serves, in finding my own truth. At the end of the day, it's all housekeeping.

They say when a door closes, a window opens. What they don't say is that the new view may not be what you expected. My new husband does not care a thing about the beach, the ocean, or East Hampton, though he does love our friends there. After ten days or so, the mountains and California call him home. His lack of enthusiasm for East Hampton, however, does not diminish my own. The house is too small for him, but he appreciates what I've created, and he gets that I need time to be there. I love him for that.

It is one of life's greatest reliefs—right up there with the ending of your child's school play—to realize that no one person or relationship can fulfill all your needs, much less mirror them. Just as no one person, situation, thing, or house will make you "happy," as if happiness were an egg that hatches when you pick the right nest.

Simone de Beauvoir wrote, "The ideal of happiness has always taken material form in the house, whether cottage or castle. It stands for permanence and separation from the world." Yet while the ideal is ephemeral, the metaphor is enduring. The house, whether cottage or castle, stands for who we are, how we live, and how we love ourselves and others. I wish for you a home you can be yourself in, and a self you can be at home in.

The end,

for now.

Acknowledgments

Gratitude, they say, is good for you. Thank goodness for that, because I am overflowing with it right about now. So many people helped make this little book happen, starting with Stephen Drucker and then Newell Turner, who, as successive editors-in-chief of *House Beautiful* magazine championed the column, "The Makeover of Bee Cottage." Thanks, also, to Shax Riegler and to David Murphy at *HB* who shepherded it along. To Trevor Tondro for his beautiful photographs. Ditto to Tria Giovan.

A while back, *House Beautiful* and *FrancesSchultz.com* reader Leslie Basham wrote me a lovely note about the magazine column. On the back of the envelope she wrote "You should write a book about Bee Cottage." I still have it. Thank you, dear Leslie.

A huge thank you to John Tomko of Rain Management Group, and to Beth and Tricia Davey of Davey Literary & Media, who got me where I needed to be (when I wasn't on a plane going somewhere else—lol). To the talented and unflappable Janice Shay of Pinafore Press, whose design of this book truly brings it to life. You all were so wonderful to work with, I don't even know where to start. Let's do another!

To Julie Ganz of Skyhorse Publishing for saying yes to a project that that is neither fish nor fowl, and who yet believed it would swim and fly.

Stephen Drucker (again), Frank Newbold, and Valerie Smith deserve their own paragraph at the very least. Their guidance, support, and generosity in sharing resources were, and are, invaluable. I treasure your friendship. Thank you.

For building, plumbing, heating, painting, planting, handymanning, and slip-covering Bee Cottage and garden: Victor Aguilar, the Awning Company, Andrew Graham of Celtic Stone, Island Gunite Swimming Pools, Lillie Irrigation, Marek Janota, Kevin MacFarlane, Joe Marciniak and sons, Seila Mejia, Basilio Parada, Elga Petite, Gerardo Salinas, and Wainscott Farms.

Well done. I hope you are as proud of you as I am proud of you.

To Jane Lappin of Wainscott Farms, your garden is one of my greatest joys and brings joy to all who enter it. I am grateful for that every day.

To my neighbors, Geoffrey Garrett and Jacques Minou, Mitten and Styvie Wainwright, and Sandy and Mike McManus, thank you for being there. I am always happy to see you.

Tom Samet is Chapter 19, enough said, but a bold-faced footnote there is Tom's partner Nathan Wold. Nathan came on the scene a year or so after we started work on Bee. Nathan and Tom are a formidable team, and I don't think either of them has sat still for more than 20 seconds in their entire collective lives. I am so grateful for you both, thank you.

There is a special group of people sort of behind the scenes who do much of what in turn allows me to do what I do. Diana Harty, Gina Stollerman, Christine Cunningham, Perfect Boto, Stephanie Valentine, and Wyatt Cromer. To my husband and dear family near and far, thank you for everything you do and are. Thank you, too, dear Rosana Grannum.

To Shelly Branch, who got me thinking about decorating with Mama's things and helped me turn it into an article by that very title in *The Wall Street Journal*. The sense and sentiment of that piece echo throughout this book.

To Don and Mike Citarella of era404 Creative Group who design and maintain my website. They are bound to have a guaranteed place in heaven.

John Oetgen has been part of every design project and, like, my life, since about 1992. His spirit and knowledge are everywhere in this house.

Early readers whose friendship and advice I value tremendously are Alex Hitz, Duvall Fuqua, Nina Griscom, and Sarah Hanner.

To my healers and teachers at a vulnerable if not fraught time in my life, you have made all the difference: Dr. Maria Theodoulou, Anna Schalk, Dona Montarelli, Christel Nani, Rebecca Grace, Marge Piccini, and Sheliaa Hite.

To Anthony Gerard, my abiding affection, admiration, and respect. To Rupert and John Ge-